T0289493

START
GROW
SELL

JURGEN INGELS

50
LESSONS
FOR SUCCESSFUL
ENTREPRENEURSHIP

Lannoo
Campus

This book was originally published as
50 lessen voor ondernemers, LannooCampus, 2020.

D/2020/45/594 – ISBN 978 94 014 7413 9 – NUR 801

COVER DESIGN Gert Degrande | De Witlofcompagnie
INTERIOR DESIGN LetterLust | Stefaan Verboven
TRANSLATION Ian Connerty
PHOTO FRONT COVER Dieter Telemans

LannooCampus Publishers is a subsidiary of Lannoo Publishers,
the book and multimedia division of Lannoo Publishers nv.

LannooCampus Publishers
Vaartkom 41 box 01.02
3000 Leuven
Belgium
www.lannoocampus.com

P.O. Box 23202
1100 DS Amsterdam
Netherlands

Contents

Introduction

I started my entrepreneurial journey at a very early age – from necessity! When I was sixteen years old, I began to discover the local party scene. My father said it was okay to go, but I had to be back home by midnight. I tried to explain to him that parties actually start (and not end) at midnight and that all my other friends were allowed to stay out much later. But he wouldn't hear a word of it.

My father was a fantastic man. He had never been given the chance to study, but he was intelligent and well read. He knew a lot and always encouraged my brother and me to work hard at school and to look at the world critically. He understood that the life of an ordinary worker is not always an easy or enjoyable one. 'You'll get nowhere without hard work' was one of his favorite sayings. It was something that has always stayed with me.

He was strict. Arriving home just a minute late meant that you were grounded for the following week. And he applied his rule both systematically and progressively. I soon realized that he wasn't going to budge: if I wanted to spend more time at parties, I would need to do some pretty creative thinking. The answer came to me in a flash: what if I was the one organizing the party? That way, I would have to stay to the end, if only to clean up and lock up. I couldn't leave that in someone else's hands, could I?

Besides, there were a thousand-and-one other aspects to organizing a party that I needed to attend to: finding sponsors, managing the budget, arranging the marketing, designing the posters and getting them printed, persuading friends to help out, selling the tickets, etc. I placed my hope on the argument that organizing parties would teach me a lot about entrepreneurship – and it worked. My father finally agreed.

Our first party was called 'After Hours'. It was a big hit and before we knew it, we were organizing more and more parties each month. We eventually reached the point when we were holding a party a week and the number of people attending began to soar. We had become a small business! Fortunately, back in those days there was no such thing as 'accounts' in the party world and most payments were made under rather than over the table. We knew no better.

When I went to university, I started my studies as an industrial engineer, but I never really enjoyed it. I was more interested in history, psychology, economics and philosophy. After two years, I decided that a dramatic change of course was needed. Some people thought that I had gone crazy – something that people would often think later on as well, during my entrepreneurial career – but my mind was made up and my parents supported my decision.

It can't have been easy for them. We were not a rich family and financial sacrifices had to be made to allow two children to study at university. It was eventually agreed that I would switch to political and social sciences at what was then the UFSIA, which is now part of the University of Antwerp. To help pay for it all, I combined my studies with a 30-hour week working in a Quick burger bar. I lost count of the number of burgers I cooked and I can safely say that Giant holds no secrets for me!

If you are working thirty hours a week, it is impossible to attend all your lectures and lessons. Thankfully, I had lots of good friends who diligently took notes for me. Some of them even jotted down the jokes (mostly bad) that the professors had told. I quickly realized that these notes were worth their weight in gold – and not just for me. In return for a free Quick meal, I got the necessary permission to commercialize them. Once again, what started as a necessity had turned into an opportunity. It was to become a recurrent theme in my later entrepreneurial career.

I found someone to type out the notes and made a good deal with a local computer store. They had just taken over a copy center, but didn't really know what use to make of all their photocopy machines. I paid them two eurocents for every copied page of notes, which I then sold to my fellow students for four cents a page. A good margin, don't you think?

I started with notes for the various political and social sciences courses I was studying but soon branched out into other courses, such as applied economic sciences and law. More were destined to follow.

Later, I added exam questions to my 'range' of products. In return for a pint (or two) in a local pub, I persuaded students to tell me what questions they had just been asked by the examiners. Once again, I had these typed up and made available to everyone – for a small fee. Because professors tend to ask the same things with almost predictable regularity, I soon had a list of nearly all the possible exam questions for every subject. Handy for myself, but also handy for my friends.

Before I had finished studying, my 'company' had sold more than a million copies. After I graduated, I bequeathed it to the student faculty. Above all, it taught me how you can place a product in the market by word-of-mouth advertising.

During my second year at university, I was chosen as president of the faculty and chairman of the student union. Thanks to my sale of course notes and exam questions, I no longer needed to work as many hours at the Quick so I had more time on my hands. The Political and Social Sciences Faculty was one of the smallest and poorest in the entire university. The parties organized by the faculty never drew in more than a few hundred people and in general 'pol and soc' students tended to be regarded as weirdos. 'Time for a change,' I thought.

And thus the *Nacht van de Erotiek* was born. This event – the name translates roughly as 'Erotic Nights' – was an attempt to focus on the risk of HIV, but in a fun way. A pair of strippers soon got the party atmosphere going, but it was all fairly innocent, certainly in comparison with the kinds of things you can see on television nowadays.

Be that as it may, back then it was enough to spread the name and fame of our faculty throughout the city and beyond. We were no longer the weirdos; we were now the talk of the town. Suddenly, everyone wanted tickets to our parties, which did our finances no harm at all. Almost overnight, we were transformed from one of the poorest faculties in the university into one of its richest. My lessons this time? That you can always win, even from an underdog position, and that creativity and imagination are powerful weapons.

The *Nacht van de Erotiek* might have been popular with my fellow students, but it didn't make me popular with the university authorities. In particular, the rector, a male version of Queen Victoria, was not amused. He had a problem with the basic concept, no matter how hard I tried to explain that the main aim was to promote an important campaign about the safe use of condoms.

To polish up my tarnished reputation, but also because I like organizing events, during my studies for my Master of Business Administration (MBA) degree, I tried out a new concept: ClassX. The basic idea was that we would arrange a concert for young people with the Philharmonic Orchestra of Flanders. There was, however, a special element: all the profits would be invested in the purchase of 2,000 bottles of champagne, which everyone could drink to their heart's content at the reception after the concert. This reception was actually a huge networking event that would allow the sponsoring companies to come into contact with the attending students, which was potentially interesting for both groups' futures. Once again, this convinced me of the power of networking, so much so, that we organized this event several times, even after I had finished my studies.

During my MBA, I had to undertake a period of on-the-job training. I was sent to work at the Gemeentekrediet, a financial institution that later became part of the Dexia banking group. In 1996, Gemeentekrediet had plans to set up a large risk capital fund. Two other students and I were given the task of finding the evidence to substantiate scientifically that this was a brilliant idea.

It soon became clear that the bank didn't have the faintest idea about risk capital and what it involved. In fact, they had very little experience at all of dealing with companies and investments. They weren't that kind of bank. As a result, instead of backing the management proposal, we argued that it was better to set up a much smaller fund that would allow Gemeentekrediet to ease its way gently into the unpredictable world of risk investment.

We took something of a gamble, because our task had simply been to find substantiating elements to support the idea, not to revise it completely. But I wasn't prepared to substantiate something that I knew was not really in the interests of the bank.

After we had made our presentation to the senior management committee and answered their barrage of questions, the bank finally agreed with our point of view and I was given the opportunity to set up the small fund we had recommended. There was just one problem: my work at the bank had given me some first insights into risk capital, but I was by no means a specialist.

To overcome this problem, I asked two of my younger friends to write their thesis on the subject of risk capital. 'Search throughout Europe for all the possible information you can find about risk capital funds.' That was their task. *How do these funds work? What structures do they use? How do they make their decisions?* I wanted to know everything.

After just a few months, they had provided me with a mine of valuable information. Because they were students, the banks had given them everything they asked for: specimen contracts, details of operational organization, criteria for analysis, etc. By the end of six months, we had acquired a level of knowledge that would have taken us five or six years to acquire organically. Just as importantly, I learned how you can reduce the duration of a project and quickly become your own expert.

For the next five years or so, I did my work with great passion. I was responsible for investing money in young technology companies in exchange for shares, with the aim of then later selling those shares for profit, both in Europe and the United States. After a time, however, I found myself confronted by an interesting problem.

When we were investing in the US, it was amazingly difficult to get money transferred into our American bank account. Not only did the money take weeks to arrive, but the whole process was expensive in terms of the fees and commission charged. Once we were even told that our money was 'lost somewhere in the system'. When I asked a member of the bank staff where exactly in the system, she replied, 'I haven't got the faintest idea. You've just got to wait and pray that it turns up again.'

This financial system was a kind of black box: you knew when the capital was sent but you never knew when it was going to arrive at its final destination. I was convinced that there must be a better way of doing things and so I began to look more deeply into the processes of making international payments. I have always been inquisitive by nature and in my opinion that is something that all entrepreneurs have in common. One of my favorite questions has always been: 'Why is that so?'

It soon became clear to me that the payment infrastructure was a tangled mess of complicated procedures, a kind of financial spaghetti: details were spread across different locations, several of the processes were duplicated unnecessarily, and the real-time handling of funds was still light years away.

The more I looked at the problem, the more I became convinced that I had been presented with an opportunity to provide a solution. In my favorite pub, the Rond Vierkant (Round Square) in Antwerp, I designed a first draft of this solution on the back of a beer mat. No rocket science, but a pragmatic way to solve the problem that no one (seemingly) had yet thought of.

A new idea was born. I took advantage of the bank's career interruption program and set about developing my solution. Looking back, it was a crazy decision. I knew nothing about payment systems. And I can still vividly remember a conversation I had with a manager in the bank's payment department about the merits of my new brainchild: 'We've been doing things the same way for the past twenty years and it works. Why the hell would we want to change it?'

Kimball Felix, a good friend of mine, became my first employee. At the time, he was working at what was then Citibank but he was bored out of his mind. I convinced him to join my adventure. At this point, we felt we needed a name. What did we want to do? We wanted to make and clear payments. And so we became Clear2Pay! All dreamt up over a couple of bottles of good wine. I can still hear my wife's comment during our brainstorming session: 'Boys and their toys!' It was only later that I came to realize the importance of having a good international name.

Clear2Pay eventually grew into a multinational company with more than 20 offices worldwide, employing 1,200 people and providing software to 40 of the 50 largest banks in the world, including the Federal Reserve Bank, the Bank of China, and Wells Fargo.

It was a marvelous adventure. Sometimes there were triumphs; sometimes there were setbacks. Sometimes there was joy; sometimes there was frustration. We attracted risk capital and took over one company after another. We had fun but we also had plenty of anxious moments. Managers were hired and fired. Along the way, I learned that money sometimes brings out the worst in people.

At the end of 2014, this adventure came to an end. We sold Clear2Pay to FIS, a large American technology company. Some people thought that Clear2Pay was just a lucky shot on our part. I knew that they were wrong, precisely because I had personal experience of just how hard it is to get a technology company off the ground and then keep it in the air. Of course you need luck, but I believe that there are also certain methods you need to apply in order to maximize your chances of success. For this reason, ever since 2014 I have been involved in the setting up and running of new technology companies, in part to prove that Clear2Pay was anything but a lucky shot. My aim was, and is, to show that it is perfectly possible to develop a successful tech-company from a base in Flanders, a region that has good engineers, a high standard of living, and housing that is much cheaper than in cities like Amsterdam or London.

One of the companies that I have helped to grow is Guardsquare. This Leuven-based enterprise creates software to protect the source code of your mobile devices against hackers. The company was chosen as 'Scale-up of the Year' in 2019, exactly ten years after Clear2Pay won the same prize. In addition to Guardsquare, I am also involved in Silverfin, BrightAnalytics, Projective, and Deliverect. These are all companies about which we will hear great things in the future, of that I am certain. In addition, to provide a better framework for investment and also because I think there are simply too few Flemish technology funds, I decided to set up a new investment fund of my own, SmartFin, with a good friend. It was a new adventure, starting again from scratch. And once again, it was a bull's-eye. SmartFin now manages some 300 million euros of funds.

SmartFin has already realized two highly successful Flemish exits: the introduction of Materialise (3D-printing) on NASDAQ, the American technology stock exchange, and the sale of Newtec (satellite communication) to ST Engineering. These two exits have made it possible to further expand the fund, allowing us to invest in a growing number of technology players.

However, I want to do much more than simply invest money in companies. I also want to inspire people. I want to enthuse others with my burning passion for entrepreneurship and technology. As a young boy, I once visited the Flanders Technology International trade fair, where I goggled in amazement at all the different robots and other clever ideas on show. As an adult, I thought it was a pity that this kind of major technology festival was no longer organized in Flanders. There are plenty of such festivals in other countries, including Slush (Helsinki) and Web Summit (Lisbon). I contacted various bodies to see if they were interested in organizing something similar in Flanders. They all said they would think about it and get back to me. Six months later, they were still thinking ...

As a result, in 2018 I decided to do it myself, working together with a few friends who are all as crazy as I am. In just a few months' time we had SuperNova up and running, a technology festival with guest speakers from around the world and a wide selection of demonstrations to provide inspiration in dozens of different fields. There was a section with things of interest for companies, but also a section for the general public.

The idea to organize the festival might have been impulsive, but the outcome was fantastic. We were able to welcome no fewer than 35,000 visitors to various locations in Antwerp. And it gave me great pleasure to receive hundreds of positive reactions. This made it clear to me that we had a good basis for organizing something similar again in the future.

Inspiring people and sharing my knowledge is also something that I have been able to do through my participation in the Belgian version of the *Shark Tank* (USA) or *Dragons' Den* (Britain) TV program. The basic idea is that budding entrepreneurs try to sell their ideas to a panel of investors, in the hope of being given the necessary financial support to turn their ideas into practical reality. I was one of the investors and I had great fun during the recording sessions. It was great to experience the passion and the fire that I saw in the eyes of some of the participants. But what struck me most was the realization that an awful lot of work still needs to be done to teach potential entrepreneurs how to pitch successfully. It was clear that many of them lacked even minimum knowledge about finance, sales and internationalization.

Since the sale of Clear2Pay, I have been asked time and again to reveal the secret of how you can develop a major company when starting from almost nothing. Sadly, and to the disappointment of many, I always have had to reply that there is no secret, no magic formula. You can only draw conclusions and learn lessons from your own experience and the experience of others.

This book describes a number of the most important of these lessons. If my children should ever consider becoming entrepreneurs, then I hope that this is the first book they will consult. It will give them a necessary push in the back and help them to overcome the obstacles they will undoubtedly face.

Every entrepreneur follows a different path and there are many paths that can lead to success. I am certainly not claiming that my wisdom is the only wisdom or that I have a monopoly on the truth. That is not the purpose of this book. It is simply a succession of my own personal experiences and anecdotes that may prove useful and inspirational to other budding entrepreneurs in their efforts to make their own dreams come true.

Here's to the crazy ones, the misfits,
the rebels, the troublemakers, the round
pegs in the square holes ... the ones
who see things differently — they're
not fond of rules ... You can quote them,
disagree with them, glorify or vilify
them, but the only thing you can't do
is ignore them because they change
things ... they push the human race
forward, and while some may see them
as the crazy ones, we see genius,
because the ones who are crazy
enough to think that they can change
the world, are the ones who do.

– Steve Jobs

1 $(1.01)^{365} = 37.78$

I have already said it in the introduction, but it needs to be repeated: there is no secret recipe or golden tip to becoming a successful entrepreneur. There is, however, a neat mathematical formula to which I often refer when I am questioned (as I frequently am) on this subject. It is a pearl of wisdom that I have applied since my student days and that has also helped me a lot as an entrepreneur. In fact, it has never let me down. I have even given it a name: 'the power of the extra mile'.

To understand this mathematical rule, you need grasp the significance of the following three calculations:

$(1.00)^{365} = 1.00$

$(1.01)^{365} = 37.78$

$(0.99)^{365} = 0.03$

The first figure varies in each case by just one-hundredth. One percent. A negligible amount, you might think. Until you exponentially multiply it by the number of days in a year. All of a sudden that single hundredth makes a huge difference.

In the past, I have applied this mathematical metaphor in various ways. When I was at university, I was the member of a student club called 'Westlandia'. When it came to partying and drinking, we had a certain reputation in Antwerp that we were expected to uphold. Our 'cantus' were famous (or rather notorious) throughout the city and every evening you could find us downing pint after pint in our regular pub.

Many of my fellow students, who were either not members of a club or else belonged to a club that took things a bit easier than we did, thought there was no earthly chance that I would ever pass my exams and get my degree. But what they failed to see was that every day – before I went to the pub – I studied hard for a couple of hours. I began this habit on the very first day of the academic year and kept it up right to the very end. I never missed a day.

Two hours a day doesn't sound like very much, but as a student it will get you a hell of a long way. It allows you to build up a good lead over the students who only begin their serious studying during the pre-exam revision period. This is what I mean by the power of the extra mile: it is the bonus of consistently doing that little bit more than everyone else.

As an entrepreneur, I am regularly asked how I manage to combine all the different activities of all the different companies with which I am involved. Once again, the answer is to be found in the power of the extra mile in that simple mathematical formula. For example, I often work on Saturday mornings, from nine to twelve. It is just three hours a week, but if you add up all those three-hour periods over the course of a year, you end up with an additional twenty or so working days. Almost a full extra month. Imagine what you could achieve if you had your own thirteenth month!

Even as a student, I understood that micro-progress is also a form of progress. In fact, micro-progress is a necessary prerequisite for moving forward at all. 'Mighty oaks from little acorns grow' is the essence of the formula that has been my guide for the past thirty years. Big things are often made from a succession of little ones.

Building up a company is like having to climb a huge mountain. When you look at the mountain from a distance and realize that you somehow have to get to the top of it, you may sometimes lose heart. As a result, many people decline to take on the challenge. They are afraid of the mountain, frightened of its size or fearful that they don't have the right tools and expertise to tackle it. Whereas in reality, conquering the mountain is very simple: if you take enough small steps in the right direction, sooner or later you will arrive at the summit. Entrepreneurship is just as simple: it requires you to consistently take a new step forward each day. Sometimes it might only be a little step; but sometimes it might suddenly be a huge one.

My mathematical formula works in both directions. Just as it is possible to make spectacular progress with no more than one percent of extra effort each day, so it is possible to lose ground in equally spectacular fashion with one percent less effort. I often meet people who seem to expect that they can achieve more by doing less. Nothing could be further from the truth. The vast majority of the successful entrepreneurs I know – including the brilliant geniuses who are always bursting with new ideas – have only been able to reach the top because they were willing to apply the philosophy of the extra mile.

$(1.01)^{365} = 37.78$

2   Entrepreneurs peak around the age of 45[1]

I was 28 years old when I started with Clear2Pay. It was the first company of my own, but I was no longer wet behind the ears. I had the big advantage that I had already been through a crash course in entrepreneurship. The bank where I worked had given me plenty of freedom. It specialized in loans to local authorities and institutions of one kind or another but had very little prior experience of dealings with companies. This was now my task and they gave me the necessary space to do my own thing. I had already started up a new department for this purpose and I had a seat on the boards of several of the companies in which we invested. These were all fast growers from different sectors, some of them active outside of Belgium.

There is no age limit on good ideas. You are never too old or too young to have them. But without my experience as an investment manager I would never have been able to overcome the obstacles with which I was confronted during the early period of Clear2Pay. Even with that experience, the start-up and development of the company was a hell of a ride!

A few years ago, the Massachusetts Institute of Technology (MIT), one of the most prestigious technical universities in the world, conducted a major study into entrepreneurship. Amongst other things, the researchers wanted to identify the ideal age for starting up a company. At what age were the chances of success the greatest?

There is a popular misconception that young entrepreneurs are the most successful ones. A young 23-year-old wolf is bursting with energy, does not yet have a family to distract him, and has the guts to take risks. Or so this theory goes. But are those really the keys to entrepreneurial success? The MIT study concluded that they are not. In fact, the study suggested that it the 45-year-old entrepreneurs who have the biggest chance of success, not the 23-year-olds. By the time they are in their mid-forties, entrepreneurs have more financial resources, more experience and a larger network. Above all, it is this final asset that is worth its weight in gold.

Many of my friends are forty-somethings. They often have good ideas for starting up a company. Many of them even have a fully developed business plan, supported by a battery of incontrovertible facts and figures and extensive market research.

But if I ask them what is holding them back, they always have an excuse for doing nothing: 'I am too old', 'I have a good steady job', 'I'm not good enough', 'I need to pay the mortgage', 'I have missed my opportunity', and on and on. Once again, nothing could be further from the truth.

Entrepreneurs are at their best after their fortieth birthday. They just need to have the courage to take the plunge. Joggers will be familiar with the phrase: 'The hardest steps you take are the steps to your own front door.' It is the same with entrepreneurship. Of course, this does not mean that you should start your entrepreneurial adventure recklessly, heedless of the risks. But if you have a good idea and a good plan, don't be afraid to give it a shot.

And if things don't work out the way you hoped? At worst, you will be an experience richer. An experience that will increase your value in the labor market. Or perhaps an experience, now that you have the taste for it, that will encourage you to have a second try.

As Mark Twain once wrote, 'Twenty years from now, you will be more disappointed by the things you didn't do than by the ones you did do.'

1 Azoulay, P., Jones, B., Kim, J., Miranda, J. (2018, 11 July). Research: The average age of a successful startup founder is 45. https://hbr.org/2018/07/research-the-average-age-of-a-successful-startup-founder-is-45

Age is something
that doesn't
matter, unless you
are cheese.

– Billie Burke

3   Think before you act

Every company works with annual targets: X percent growth, X million euros revenue, X million euros profit, etc. Everyone in the company needs to be aware of these targets. Achieving them is often linked to rewards, such as bonuses, stock options, or commissions.

Many companies now link these targets to incentives for the entire organization, for all the employees together. They shut up shop for a few days and head off to some pleasant location where they can mix business with pleasure. This kind of trip is the ideal moment for discussing the strategy for the coming year, providing you don't overdo it. The intention is that the trip should be a reward – and very few people regard three days of non-stop strategic meetings as a reward!

In many companies, and especially in companies that are growing fast, many of the employees only know each other superficially. Spending a few days together can work wonders for the cohesion of your organization and for its internal communication. Group activities strengthen team spirit. The tall stories told at the bar or around the campfire and the few beers that get tongues wagging extend this bonding process deep into the evening and night.

A few years ago, one of the companies I am involved in managed to achieve a truly amazing revenue figure. The target for that year was already so high that few of the managers and even fewer of the staff thought that it was attainable. But thanks to everyone's hard work, we exceeded our wildest expectations. This was a performance that deserved something in return – and that something was a trip to the wonderful city of Rome. Our first evening ended with everyone drinking too much *vino* in a local wine bar. Arriving back in our hotel rooms, we all found a white or black t-shirt waiting for us, with the instruction to wear it the next morning.

There were plenty of hangovers in evidence at the breakfast table. Even so, after a good meal and several cups of coffee, our two teams – one black and one white – set off for a large lake just outside of Rome. There we saw two large boats, each in a different color and each beautifully decorated with a dragon's head at the prow. These boats were really open canoes, fourteen meters long and a meter wide, and it soon became clear that the two teams were going to race each other in them. There was room for sixteen paddlers and one captain.

Working together is often more important for winning this kind of race than individual strength. To generate top speed, the paddles need to enter and leave the water at exactly the same moment. In this respect, dragon boat racing is the ultimate team sport.

An enthusiastic old rower explained to us the best paddling techniques. He also told us that the Chinese had been winning races in these boats for centuries, humiliating the opposition, European and American alike, even with crews containing Olympic rowers, sailors, and others with significant water sports experience. And all because the Chinese worked together with streamlined perfection.

It was agreed that our two teams would race each other twice, with a final deciding race if there was a tie. I was in the black boat and I could see that our opponents were raring to go. They had already chosen a battle cry and they sprinted down to the waterside for a quick practice before the first race. They appointed a captain, took up their positions in the boat and distributed the various tasks among themselves with an almost military precision.

Having seen all this, I didn't give our team much chance of winning. Purely by chance, the CEO – who had arranged the distribution of the black and white t-shirts – wound up with all the sportiest members of staff on his own white team. They looked across at our black boat with something like disdain. You could see them thinking: 'No contest!'

The practice session seemed to bear this out. The white captain set the tempo by counting – 'One, two, three' – and the paddles flashed in and out of the water at what seemed to be lightning speed. But we soon noticed that their tempo began to splutter, precisely because of the captain's way of counting. If one of the rowers was slower, this ruined the rhythm of all the others. To remain in unison, you need to remain super-focused and we understood that the captain's counting was breaking his crew's concentration. There was just too much time between each number he counted.

If you are not strong, you need to be smart. And our team was not strong. Consequently, we agreed to count in series of ten, always using the word 'and' between each number: 'And one, and two, and three ...' What's more, we said that everyone in the boat had to count together out loud and that the paddle should be removed from the water between strokes on the 'and'. Once we put this system into practice, we were surprised at our own speed. Having established this, we decided to save our strength for the races, while watching our opponents continue to practice like lunatics: lots of effort, lots of noise, lots of posturing, but no analysis and no strategy.

We won the first race, much to the surprise and frustration of the white boat. They were convinced that our victory was a fluke and that they would crush us in the second race. But they didn't. We won that one as well, by a margin of two clear lengths. There was no decider necessary. Our triumph was complete!

The moral of the story? We won the race because we first thought about a strategy and only then moved on to its execution. The white boat did exactly the opposite. This is a wise lesson for anyone interested in entrepreneurship. You will often hear it said in the business world that 'It's all in the execution', and of course this is true. But that doesn't mean that you should charge at your entrepreneurial dream like a bull at a gate. Don't waste valuable time unnecessarily, but make sure you take enough time to think about the best approach for achieving the results you desire.

Entrepreneurship is an awful lot like dragon boat racing. So is it really a surprise that China is often ahead of us in both fields?

4   Entrepreneurship in the blood

People often ask me about the qualities that make a good entrepreneur. As I mentioned in the introduction, I had already caught the entrepreneurial bug when I was relatively young. To talk about people being 'born entrepreneurs' may sound like a bit of a cliché, but like most clichés there is a good deal of truth in it. Of course, there are certain things that you can learn along the way, but without having entrepreneurship in your blood you will find the journey a lot harder.

In my case, this entrepreneurial blood has always flowed through my veins at top speed. When my children were small, like all children they needed disposable nappies. I remember thinking at the time that these nappies were hugely expensive. When I heard that a German company had gone bust, I decided to buy up a full shipping container of their remaining nappy stock. I organized the transport and stored the nappies in our attic. News that I had a nappy hoard quickly spread, first throughout our street and then throughout the rest of the village. As a result, a growing number of people came to buy their nappies from me. I was soon known as 'nappy man'! Even today, many years later, people still occasionally stop me in the supermarket to ask if I am still selling nappies. Sadly, I have to disappoint them. However, I later made similar 'misuse' of our attic for another of my entrepreneurial adventures, when I purchased 12,000 coconut bowls from Thailand. During our visit to the country I wanted to show some concrete support of the local population and buying the bowls seemed like a good way to do it. Half the attic is still full of them, so if you know of anyone who needs a coconut bowl (or preferably a lot of coconut bowls), you know where to find me. The moral of this story? I truly believe that entrepreneurs are born, and not made. It is something that is in you and that you cannot resist.

Of course, to talk about a 'born entrepreneur' sounds pretty vague. So let's look at things a little more closely. What are the key components that go into making entrepreneurial blood?

Passion

Passion is far and away the most crucial characteristic. You have to have the sacred fire within you. All good entrepreneurs are passionate about their product, their service or their company. They never tire of talking about these things, and you can almost see their eyes sparkle with enthusiasm as they do it. If you don't have this passion, there isn't really much point in trying to become an entrepreneur. You will never make it.

Persistence

Second on the list is persistence. No company makes it straight to the top in an unbroken line of success. Inevitably, there are ups and downs. As a result, there are also alternating periods of euphoria and disappointment. In fact, you can sometimes feel both in the same working day. At some point, every company goes through stormy waters, and problems often blow up from where you least expect them.

I experienced this first hand during the banking crisis of 2008. There were times when we were perilously close to bankruptcy. Most of our clients were financial institutions and during the crisis they stopped paying their bills from one day to the next.

As a result, no money was coming into the company, but we still needed to pay our employees at the end of each month. It was touch and go, but fortunately we were able to rely on our shareholders. For me, this was an important lesson. If we hadn't kept on believing, it could have been the end of the story for Clear2Pay.

Dynamism – or the urge to act

Lots of people have brilliant ideas, which they talk about and play with year after year, without ever doing anything concrete about it. For me, the essence of entrepreneurship is taking action.

Of course, you need to think carefully before you start up your company, but actually starting it is the most important thing. Once you have done this, the rest will follow. I often meet people who claim that they had a fantastic idea and

could have had a flourishing company. Could have, should have, would have ...
Words, like ideas, are nothing without the action to back them up.

As an entrepreneur, you have to have the courage to take a leap of faith into
the dark. What distinguishes entrepreneurs from others is not their ideas, but
their willingness to put those ideas into practice. At a certain moment, they
stop thinking, discussing and planning – and they act.

Luck

Every entrepreneur needs his or her portion of luck. Having the gods on your
side is a factor that should not be underestimated. In the entrepreneurial world,
the difference between success and failure is often very small. Seemingly minor
details can sometimes be decisive. Having a bit of luck at the right moment can
tip the balance in your favor.

It was no different for us at Clear2Pay. We were lucky to come into contact with
the right person in Visa at just the right time, someone who understood our
vision and was prepared to take the risk of collaborating with a small company
like ours. Every entrepreneur – even the biggest and the best – needs a lucky
break every now and then.

Curiosity

When I started Clear2Pay, I knew nothing about the payments market. But I
was inquisitive and willing to learn. I read all the articles I could find and talked
with all the people who could help me increase my knowledge. If you devote
yourself fully to a subject for a couple of months, you often find that you end
up knowing more than the so-called 'experts'. People like to use jargon to give
the impression that things are more complex than they really are. In reality,
nothing could be further from the truth.

As far as payments were concerned, I quickly made up my lost ground on the
'experts', simply because I was hungry to learn. I threw myself wholeheartedly
into a new market and wanted to know everything about it. As an entrepreneur,
this is the kind of curiosity you must have.

The rebellious spirit

To be a good entrepreneur, you need to be a bit of rebel. Don't listen too much to those around you who say what you should or shouldn't do. Entrepreneurship means taking risks – and that is something that most people are not comfortable with.

Countless prospective entrepreneurs have failed to live their dream, simply because they were put off by the 'good advice' of their family and friends. 'You realize that you won't have an income if you fall ill?' 'What about your pension?' 'Surely you're not going to give up your well-paid job at the multinational?' Don't listen to them! Believe in yourself and resist the temptation of the golden cage. Go full steam ahead – and don't look back.

Turning your passion
into your job is
easier than finding
a job that matches
your passion.

– *Seth Godin*

5   Slower. Less. Costlier.

Every year I read a couple of hundred business plans. The quality can vary considerably. My tip? Dear entrepreneurs, hire the services of a good copywriter. It doesn't cost very much and at the very least he or she can weed out all the spelling mistakes. Yet notwithstanding the variation in quality, there is one thing that all these plans have in common: the bottom line is always wildly optimistic. Always.

By definition, entrepreneurs are optimists – otherwise, they wouldn't want to start a business. But that optimism sometimes gets in the way of their making an accurate assessment of their potentiality.

Over the years, I have discovered a number of patterns and laws that help me to evaluate all those business plans realistically.

In my experience, the revenues are always generated later than the prognosis suggests and always at a significantly lower level. I assume a delay of two financial quarters in comparison with the original plan and a reduction of twenty-five percent in the amount. This usually brings me much closer to the real situation. This correction is important for accurately estimating the cash flow and the resources that the company will need.

Entrepreneurs are impatient. For me, that's fine. I love that *sturm-und-drang* mentality. But they often forget that they are dependent on others. If you want to conclude a commercial deal with a major company, you need to take into account a long sales cycle. The internal processes that need to be completed before you can be recognized as a supplier can sometimes take months. And the bigger the company, the greater the number of departments that need to give their approval. That inevitably takes time.

In my own company I always calculated on the basis of a buffer of six months. If my CTO told me that the next release of software would be ready in Q1, I assumed it would actually be released in Q3. When my CFO swore blind that he would get the fund-raising completed in Q2, I made a mental note that the money would only be available in Q4. If the sales director predicted that he would be able to sign a major deal in the second half of the year, I knew that it would probably only take place in the first half of the following year.

Moreover, it is not only the revenue figures that are wide of the mark in these prognoses. The expenses are nearly always higher in reality than was foreseen in the original business plan. For a start-up or scale-up, it is the salaries of the staff that take the biggest bite out of the budget. Especially if the company continues to blossom and grow.

Most companies are reasonably good at estimating how many people they need. But they are less good at working out the actual cost of employing those people. You would be amazed how often budding entrepreneurs fail to correctly calculate employer taxes and contributions to employee retirement plans.

A good rule of thumb that I use to calculate the total company salary cost is to multiply the monthly gross salary cost by a factor of twenty. This means that an employee who earns a gross salary of 5,000 euros each month will cost the company around 100,000 euros over the course of a full year.

And it is not just salary costs. Other overhead costs are also frequently underestimated. Whether it is ICT, marketing, events, insurance or administrative expenditure, there is always something unexpected or something that people forget. For this reason, it is a smart move to always add thirty percent to the specific costs you have itemized in your business plan.

I apply these broad rules to all the business plans that are sent to me. I increase costs by thirty percent, lower revenues by twenty-five percent and put back all the date projections by half a year. In this way, I get a plan that will much more closely reflect reality.

In addition, I always make a spreadsheet with the figures for revenues, expenses, and salaries, which I can then vary to take account of different situations. This makes it possible for me to look at numerous possible combinations, which in turn allows me to calculate (and recalculate) the EBITDA margin and the cash flow.

Imagine that my turnover falls by ten percent and my costs increase by thirty percent. My graphic will immediately show me the effects of these changes on my EBITDA and cash flow. This is useful when you are sitting in a meeting with your investors, who are very good (and rightly so) at asking awkward questions. The ability to adjust your figures quickly and provide them with the answers they need on your screen just seconds later can make the difference between securing their approval – or not.

6   Don't throw dust in people's eyes

Entrepreneurs have the tendency to see things as being more positive than they really are. As examples, they massage the projected sales figures, bring forward (on paper, at least) the release date for the latest product variant, and advance the scheduled date for the signing of a major deal. If you see that staff, customers or investors are getting a bit restless, it is a natural human reaction to try and sell them a little bit of bluff.

And in the short-term it might actually work. But sooner or later – and usually sooner – your over-optimism and half-truths will be exposed for what they are and will come boomeranging back at you with twice the force. For this reason, it is always better to assess developments in your company as realistically as possible. In short: be honest and tell it like it is. The best strategy is to underestimate and overperform.

In this respect, I will never forget the biggest reality check that I ever experienced in my professional career. It hit me like a thunderbolt, all the more so because it came from a totally unexpected quarter.

We were in our Clear2Pay office, putting together our new Ikea furniture, when Visa called. They had read the abstract of our patent application and asked if they could come along to discuss things further. They were interested in the way we wanted to unravel the spaghetti that was tying the payments sector in knots.

At that time, Clear2Pay had a dozen or so employees who sat like sardines in a can, all packed into an office that measured no more than five meters by eight. There were pizza boxes everywhere and the walls were covered with post-it notes and 'to do' lists. In short: complete chaos.

We already had a rough first draft of how the functionality of the software should look, but we hadn't actually begun the programming work. Of course, this was something we didn't want to admit to Visa. So when they asked how far we had progressed with the programming, we told them that the first version was almost sixty percent completed. At the end of the meeting, the people from Visa said that they would be back in two months with an important delegation to take a closer look. Two months! If we worked day and night in shifts, there was just a chance that we might be able to get that sixty percent finished by the time they returned.

There was, however, one major problem: we didn't have a server on which to install and operate the software. How could we demonstrate our sixty percent if we didn't even have a server? At that time, Sun servers were the best in the business. But they cost upwards of two hundred thousand euros, whereas we could hardly pay the rent on our tiny office. Put simply, we needed to find a server and we needed to find one fast. Otherwise, we could kiss our potential deal with Visa goodbye.

An entrepreneur needs to be creative. I screwed up all my courage and picked up the phone to call Sun Belgium. Would they be prepared to lend us a server for a month or two? Because we dangled the prospect of a major deal with Visa in front of them, but also because they found us likeable (or so I prefer to think), they agreed. We were as happy as the proverbial dog with two tails. It was like Christmas had come early!

The server was delivered a few days later and deposited in the cellar of the innovation center where we had our office. It was a huge piece of equipment, with lots of flashing bits and pieces that made it look really cool. We worked around the clock to get the software ready and we were finally able to upload it onto the Sun server just 24 hours before Visa's return visit was scheduled.

This time, the Visa delegation was led by a more elderly woman. It was soon clear that she had tons of experience and had been on dozens of company visits of this kind. At one point, she asked whether she could see the server on which the software was operated. 'Of course,' we replied. We thought we were certain to make a big impression: there couldn't be too many start-ups that already had a brand new Sun server like ours! 'Have you had it for long?' she queried. 'Ages,' we replied.

When we arrived in the cellar, the woman asked for a chair to be brought. I thought that she was out of breath from the walk down the stairs and needed to recover. Imagine our surprise when she picked up the chair, placed it alongside the server and climbed on top of it, so that she could run her finger along the top of the console. No dust! In this way, she knew the server had only been recently installed and that we had been less than honest with her upstairs.

This taught me a wise lesson that I have never forgotten. Never say things or promise things that you cannot make good. There will always be someone smarter than you who will be able to see through your bluff. In spite of this error of judgment on our part, we were still able (thankfully!) to convince Visa of the merits of our software. Weeks later we signed a deal with them, our first major client and the basis of the huge worldwide success of Clear2Pay in the years that followed.

In the old days, you could sell things using just a few glossy slides and some slick sales talk. Not anymore. Nowadays, products are immediately tested to death by interested companies and they expect you to demonstrate your software either in their environment or in the cloud. The age of bluff and sleight of hand has gone forever – and it's probably a good thing, too!

7   Life is like a box of chocolates?

Not all my entrepreneurial ventures have been successful. Sometimes I have run full speed … into a brick wall. Entrepreneurship is a matter of trial and error. If you don't succeed, to use the words of the old song, you must 'pick yourself up, dust yourself off, and start all over again'. Or as Albert Einstein perhaps more elegantly expressed it: 'It is madness to do the same thing over and over again, yet still expect a different result.' He was talking about physics but it applies equally to entrepreneurship: come to terms with your failures and move on to something new.

Even so, I see far too many entrepreneurs who stick stubbornly to their original idea, convinced that sooner or later it is bound to work, when it is clear to everyone else around them that this is not going to happen.

Some time ago, a friend and I started up a chocolate shop on the market square of Roeselare, my native town in Belgium. Self-evidently, it sells blocks of chocolate and chocolate pralines, but you can also drink a cup of coffee and eat a slice of cake. As Belgium is the undisputed chocolate praline capital of the world, you might think this would be a money-maker right off the bat.

To be honest, we have had to fight for years just to break even. Even though the margin on a cup of coffee is high, you need to sell an awful lot of cups each day just to pay the wages of your staff. Unless you run the shop yourself, it is almost impossible to generate a positive cash flow, never mind earn enough to cover the initial investment costs. The fact that my mother meets there each day with her friends for a coffee and a chat is probably the only reason why I still keep the place open.

Five or so years ago, I went with the same friend on a city trip to Stockholm. Compared with Roeselare, it seemed like paradise on earth for coffee shop owners! There were coffee houses everywhere, each with its own long queue of waiting customers. In the meantime, the situation in Belgium has improved, but back then the development of a genuine coffee culture was miles ahead in Sweden.

In other words, coffee galore! But to our surprise, we saw very few shops selling chocolates. There were a few local chocolate manufacturers, but they mainly made blocks of chocolate, not the pralines for which Belgium is so internationally famous. We knew that we would need to do some confirmatory market research, but had we discovered a gap in the Swedish confectionary market? Perhaps we could make our Belgian shop indirectly more viable by opening up a shop in Stockholm?

The market research confirmed our intuition. There were relatively few competitors in the Swedish market and the local pralines (badly made, at that) cost twice as much as in Belgium, whereas on average salaries were thirty percent lower. On paper, this was a much better business case than our struggling venture in Roeselare. Consequently, we decided to convert the business case into a full-blown business plan. Every detail was covered. Nothing was left to chance. Or so we thought.

Having studied various options, we eventually decided to purchase a license to sell Leonidas chocolates in Sweden. Ten years earlier the company had tried to break into the Swedish market via a local distributer, but quickly threw in the towel. No doubt the distributer wasn't up to the job, we assumed smugly. We would do things differently – and better.

In order to be certain about the quality and the flavor of the chocolates we would need for Sweden, we organized a large-scale tasting test. We invited hundreds of Swedish men, women and children to try our pralines and the results once again confirmed our earlier suspicions: there was a large gap in the Swedish market. People loved our chocolates and price was not an issue. The Swedes wanted good chocolates and were prepared to pay for them.

We decided to go ahead with the venture and looked for a local manager/partner who could help us. Via an intermediary, we came into contact with a Swedish accountant who was looking to make a career switch. This was our first big mistake. He knew very little about running a business and we were too far away to keep a tight grip on the day-to-day operations. This is an important lesson: if you want to be involved in entrepreneurship, you cannot outsource it. Entrepreneurship is something you have to do for yourself.

Our second big mistake was to invest too much money in the interior of our first shop and not enough money in the selection of a good location. The shop looked great, but it was in an underwhelming part of town where there was too little passing trade of the right kind to buy our products. The third mistake was the fatal combination of having too much money in the local bank account and not enough control over its expenditure. Nothing is quite so easy (or so much fun) as spending other people's money – as our ex-accountant friend quickly discovered.

We probably could have corrected these three errors of judgment, if we had not made a fourth and even bigger one. Notwithstanding all our market research and the numerous test tastings, we had completely failed to understand the nature of the Swedish market. In Belgium, people buy chocolates by the half kilogram, with the intention of giving them as a present or having them to offer around when family and friends come over. After an hour, the box is already empty.

Not so in Sweden. The Swedes do not buy boxes of chocolates. They buy just one or two individual chocolates. And they don't give them as presents. Why? In Sweden, people are much more concerned about their health and there is a much closer popular association than in many other countries (including Belgium) between the consumption of chocolate and ill-health. When our first customers all purchased just a few chocolates, I immediately saw the writing on the wall. A few chocolates? Okay, that is just a little guilty pleasure. But a whole box? No way! The Swedes do not go in for that kind of excess.

Our entire business plan collapsed like a house of cards. True, we sold our pralines for only twice the normal price. But the volume was ten times lower. We had as many customers as in Belgium but sold far fewer chocolates. We had made a few minor mistakes, but we had also made a fatal one by assuming that the Swedish people would buy chocolates like the Belgians do: by the boxful. We had failed to move beyond our own normal frames of reference. We forgot that what seems normal to us in our market might seem abnormal in a market somewhere else.

By the time we fully understood this, it was too late. We already had three shops and had invested almost a million euros over a twelve-month period. However, there was no way we could ever make these shops profitable and so we were forced to close them before they lost any more money. This Swedish adventure cost me a small fortune, but I still benefit every day from the lessons it taught me.

It's fine to celebrate
success but it's more
important to heed
the lessons of failure.

– Bill Gates

8   The law of time reduction

What components do you need to build a successful company? In management books the same four elements are repeated time after time: a good team, a large market, a unique product, and money. As entrepreneur and investor, I have learned over the years that there is also a fifth element that is much more important than the other four. In fact, I would even go so far as to say that it is probably more important than the other four combined. And what is this fifth crucial success factor? Time.

To talk about time reduction sounds fairly abstract. But for me it has become a philosophy, a kind of mantra. In every company in which I am involved I always ask myself how the time factor can be reduced. What can be done faster? What can be done more efficiently?

Each hour that you can save on a particular task means an extra hour for doing something else. In this way, you can gain a lead over your competitors and ultimately be more successful. Because once you start to appreciate the crucial importance of time reduction, those hours will become days, the days will become weeks and the weeks will become months.

So how can you reduce the amount of time you need? If you look around carefully, you will soon find lots of different possibilities. Here are a few of the most important ones.

- Technology is a key factor. Consider, for example, the accounting department, which in many companies is still run the old-fashioned way with lots of manual work done manually. Technology can drastically reduce the number of hands you need for the bookkeeping, so that those hands – and the brains to which they are attached – can now be used in more profitable ways to create added value for the company. What's more, if technology makes it possible for you to close your accounts within five days of the end of each period, you get a better and a faster picture of your true financial situation, which in turn allows you to take any necessary action more quickly and more effectively.

- An Enterprise Resource Planning (ERP) system – an integrated suite of business applications – is an important instrument in any growing company. It assesses every department, attunes their operations to each other and combines them into a single streamlined flow. Selecting a good ERP system is therefore crucial. What's more, because of the importance of time reduction, the selection process itself is another area where a significant time saving can be made. Let me explain.

  Most growing companies who plan to buy an ERP system set up a work group consisting of representatives from each department. The work group then compares the available systems, asks for offers to be submitted, and eventually chooses – usually after hours and hours of discussion – the right system with the right functionalities. Once this has been done, the work group justifies its choice to management in a lengthy report. Once management is satisfied, they pass the recommendation upstairs to the board of directors, where the choice is finally approved. By this time, a year (or more) has already passed ...

  In my companies I make it a habit to reduce this selection process to a maximum time span of two months. I rely heavily on reviews and references and generally pick the supplier and the package that most other growth companies are using. Why waste your time on a long-winded selection process when there are players in the market who have earned their reputation with other rapidly expanding companies and clearly know what they are doing?

- Time reduction is also crucial in the field of recruitment. In general, it is a good idea to take on young wolves, since they are generally bursting with creativity and energy. Even so, you still need to train them and this can take quite a while. As a young and growing company, you may not be able to wait that long. Taking on people with experience can help you to reduce this training time. Agreed, you will have to pay them more, but they will be able to implement their tasks more quickly, so that you will soon win back the extra investment.

- It is even possible to reduce the time you need to acquire your external funding. If you approach an investment fund, your first point of contact will usually be someone relatively junior. If he/she regards your company as an interesting prospect, after a week or so you will eventually get an appointment with his/her boss. This process will then be repeated more than once, as you work your way up through the fund's internal hierarchy. At long last (if you are lucky), you may get to see the partner, the person who actually decides whether you get the cash (or not). With large investment funds, this is a process that can take months – valuable months that you can save if you are able to arrange a direct introduction to the partner. As a result of this shortcut, you can get that much needed injection of fresh capital much faster than you might otherwise expect.

As an entrepreneur, there are literally hundreds of ways that you can reduce time. And if you do it properly, the chances of your developing into a successful scale-up will increase exponentially. We all know the saying 'time is money'. In the digital world, this is truer than ever before.

9   Dealers and junkies

When we started with Clear2Pay, we had a clear objective in mind. We wanted to develop software that would improve the processing of payments and unravel the spaghetti that was tying bank payment procedures in knots. We also had a clear idea about the architecture of the software and its functionalities. Likewise, the proof of concept did not seem to present any major problems.

Our biggest challenge was to persuade the banks. How could we convince them not only to use our software, but also to pay a fairly hefty licensing fee for the privilege?

We had no references to offer, no reputation in the payments market and no mountains of cash to launch a slick promotion campaign. To make matters worse, our competitors were all major companies that had been active in the sector for years. We were the new kids on the block, with a cool idea but not much more than that.

As I mentioned earlier, if you are not strong, you have to be smart. I was convinced that good references were the key to getting customers over the line and generating new business. References are the jokers in the pack of a sales pitch. They can calm the fears and anxieties that potential customers experience when they are confronted with a new product or service. If they hear that companies X and Y are already using the product, their cold feet will suddenly become significantly warmer! References are crucial for building up your credibility as a company. Certainly in the banking world.

Of course, you first need to have some references before you can present them to others as proof of your brilliance. Finding a first company that is prepared to take a chance on your new idea is therefore the key to success. Once you have that first glowing reference, you can use it as a crowbar to lever open the doors to other companies. It is a kind of 'chicken-and-egg' situation. No references = no customers. But also: no customers = no references!

There was just one chance. I had a bold idea about how we could get that all-important first reference. What if we offered the use of our software free of charge to some of the banks? What's more, not just any banks, but large international banks, from whom a reference would make a big impression on other potential users.

The 'free' concept sparked off heated discussions within our team. Were we really planning to give away, free of charge, the software on which we had all worked so hard? In particular, the software engineers threatened revolution. Perhaps a price discount to convince our first few customers, but a discount of one hundred percent?! No, that was taking things too far.

In fact, I was actually proposing a discount of more than one hundred percent. I not only wanted to offer use of the software free of charge, but I was also willing to integrate it at no cost into the bank's own system. And to provide a free aftercare service.

What my team saw as a free gift, I saw as an investment. If you want to place a product in a market, you need to have the confidence to invest in it. Entrepreneurs find investments in things like development, marketing, machines and research to be self-evident. But investing in top-grade references? For some of them that seems hard to accept.

Many of the team members thought that we should focus on trying to find a first paying customer. We had already made a serious effort on the sales front and sooner or later this was bound to pay off, wasn't it? Maybe it was and maybe it wasn't, but this 'wait-and-see' approach involved a huge risk: our money was rapidly running out. We didn't have much time left.

Back then, at the end of the 1990s, the payment departments of banks were structured very differently than is the case today. They were often literally hidden away in the cellars of bank offices. Out of sight and out of mind. Their payment software was outdated in the extreme, some having been in use for more than thirty years. It was almost is if 'innovation' was a dirty word.

Most bankers failed to understand that making payments was destined to become a core activity of their profession in the near future, with important strategic value. And the people in the financial institutions who did understand this were given no budget by their superiors to improve their systems.

Because we were proposing to install our software for nothing and also invited the users to participate in the shaping of the product's road map, we quickly excited the interest of a number of large banks to participate in our 'experiment'. We were offering something new, something to break the monotony of their normal operational routine. In short, we gave the payment managers the chance to come out of their dark cellars.

Once the software was installed and running (even with only a limited functionality), the reactions from the banks were enthusiastic. They had greater insight into payment flows and the processing was much cheaper. In fact, the positive impact on their business was so great that they all wanted to hang on to our product.

You can compare our approach with that of a drug dealer who gives away a first 'taste' of an addictive drug for free, in the hope that his targets will later become paying junkies. After a time, they can no longer manage without him and in the long run they end up dealing for him as well. For us, this 'freebie' formula worked like a dream. We had the banks hooked. They were now addicted to our software.

We asked only one small favor from the banks in return for the free installation and use of our system: they had to allow us to use their names as references. This, of course, had been our purpose all along. They were the bait that we could now use to catch even bigger fish. Some bank managers almost functioned like salesmen for our product. Several even took part in sales calls, in which they told other banks just how good our software really was and how it had improved both their operational efficiency and profitability.

Whether you are a neighbor praising the virtues of the local baker to the man next door or a bank manager praising the virtues of a payment system to another bank manager, one thing is certain: no one is better at attracting new customers than an existing customer. Word-of-mouth advertising creates an unstoppable snowball effect.

In the end, we were able to convince four major reference banks on four different continents. In their own region, each of these reference banks was the absolute number one in the field of banking technology. As a result, many other banks decided to skip the testing phase for our software, trusting blindly in the recommendations of the reference banks.

What's more, these free customers quickly became paying customers as well. The range of our free functionalities was deliberately limited. We knew that once they were hooked, the banks would want to extend this range more fully. They soon began to ask us to develop or integrate new features with increasing regularity.

After just a couple of years, the amounts generated by our licensing fees were so great that no one could ever have imagined that at first we gave away our software for nothing. Our 'free' gamble had paid off and we were now firmly on the map of the banking world.

10 The super-factor

There is one factor that is crucial for entrepreneurs and overshadows all the rest. One factor that is so important that I refer to it as the super-factor. Even if you have everything perfectly under control – brilliant product, talented team, enough cash in the bank – the super-factor can still make or break your company.

To understand the significance of the super-factor, we need to take a trip through time back to the Middle Ages, when sugar was still regarded as a true delicacy. At first, sugar was only available from the apothecary's store, because people attributed so many beneficial qualities to it. In fact, it was in such short supply that you could earn a fortune if you had some. And if you could get your hands on a regular source, you were guaranteed to end up unbelievably rich.

The Italians were the first to recognize this. They developed an interesting exchange scheme for obtaining sugar from Morocco: they swapped marble, of which they had an inexhaustible supply, for the white gold. One kilogram of marble for one kilogram of sugar. The specific weight of marble is, of course, much heavier than the specific weight of sugar, so that for a single block of marble the Moroccans had to hand over a vast amount of sugar. The weight was the same, but there was a massive difference in volume.

The Italians couldn't believe their luck. They thought they had made the deal of the century! It was the medieval equivalent of winning the lottery. They were able to resell the sugar throughout Europe at hugely inflated prices. And the Moroccans? Well, at least they can still admire all the wonderful Italian marble they acquired for use in the many beautiful palaces that occupy their country.

When I was in Morocco, a local guide asked me who I thought had got the best of the deal. The Italians, whose mountains of sugar had already been consumed many centuries ago? Or the Moroccans, whose magnificent palaces continue to attract hordes of capital-rich tourists hundreds of years later?

This is a good example of the super-factor at work: it is all a matter of timing. The correct timing of a product launch is all-important. If you are too early, the market and your potential customers are not ready for your product. If you are too late, the market is already saturated, and the competition is too fierce.

In 2004, Microsoft brought a forerunner of the modern smartwatch to market. This was SPOT, one of a range of Smart Personal Objects Technology products that could send and receive data. The smartwatch could tell you all about the latest traffic jams, share prices, sports results, news, etc. But the SPOT watch never took off. People just didn't like it. The design was rudimentary and its FM frequencies had insufficient reach. It took another fifteen years before the Apple Watch, which also struggled at first, became a big success.

Another good example of timing is Friendster, the granddaddy of all social media networks. It was launched in 2002, five years before Facebook hit the scene. Friendster offered more or less the same functionalities as Facebook: it connected people online and made it possible for them to share personal messages and images. However, it had no news feed and the network experienced a number of technical problems, some of which took days to fix. It was this lack of reliability that ultimately proved fatal for Friendster – following which Facebook went on to conquer the world with a comparable but more stable platform.

Of course, there are also plenty of examples of products that were launched too late. When this happens, the market is already overloaded with similar goods, so that the level of competition is merciless. Or else your product is already outdated and has been overtaken by a better alternative.

I see many entrepreneurs who still fail to take sufficient account of this super-factor. They are so enthusiastic about their idea that they launch their product before the rest of the world is ready for it. They fail to carry out the necessary market research or neglect to think adequately about their distribution model.

Equally, I see just as many entrepreneurs who continue to develop their product beyond its reasonable life expectancy, adding one new feature after another. This not only dramatically increases their costs, but also negatively affects their market momentum.

The sugar paradox demonstrates that the same products and services can merit different prices and different levels of appreciation at different times. So it bears repeating: timing is everything. As an entrepreneur, you need to have the courage to take a long-term view. Not necessarily over a period of three hundred years, but certainly about how your market and your customers are likely to evolve in the foreseeable future. This is truer than ever before, in an era when the world can look very different just twelve months later.

The fully justified concerns about climate change are a perfect example of this. Companies that fail to play the sustainability card risk missing the boat completely – with all that this implies. Make sure that your company is not one of them.

If you're not embarrassed
by the first version of
your product, you've
launched too late.

– *Reid Hoffman*

11   Focus on your talents and waste no time on the rest

One of my female members of staff was a brilliant organizer. All kind of events were automatically handed over to her and she was guaranteed to turn them into a big success. She had a talent for organization that you seldom see.

However, she also wanted me to teach her the ins and outs of company finances. She was determined to master this aspect of the business world as well. But I knew in advance that this would be a mission impossible. No matter how hard she tried, she failed to see the important connections between the different figures. Some people have that gift; others don't. Even so, she refused to give up, so that in the end she invested a huge amount of time in something that she was not very good at.

At school and at home, we were all brought up with the idea that we should do everything possible to try and improve our results in the subjects where our performance was poor. A noble idea, of course, but the reverse side of the coin is that we spend less time on the things at which we truly excel. We work so hard to get better at things that don't suit us (and often don't even interest us) that we risk losing sight of our real passions and talents. In this way, we tend to evolve towards a kind of sterile mediocrity: bad at nothing, but good at nothing either.

If a kid comes home from school with a report that is full of As with a single D what is the typical reaction of most parents? Exactly! They congratulate the child and say that he or she has worked hard, but then add that they don't want to see that D on the next report. No child wants to disappoint his or her parents, and so the son or daughter in question will do their level best to try and turn that D into a C or B, even if the subject bores them to tears and is of little relative importance. Result: next time around the D becomes a C; but one or two of the previous As also become Bs or Cs. Is that so much better?

When I worked in a bank, like all my other colleagues, I received an annual evaluation. This was a conversation with one of my bosses that lasted about an hour. The first five minutes were usually devoted to the things that I was good at. For the remaining fifty-five minutes I was forced to listen to a monologue of my many deficiencies. Of course, I was given tips for my 'improvement' – HR had drummed into all the bank's managers that these conversations were intended to be 'constructive'.

For me, this was a pure waste of time. I knew perfectly what I did well and what I did less well. And I didn't (and still don't) have the slightest intention of doing much about the latter. For example, my French is nothing to write home about and I am a disaster when it comes to administration. To be honest, I am too impatient to be organized: I need chaos to be able to see the underlying structure. Even so, I think I can say that none of these 'defects' has prevented me from becoming a good entrepreneur, although I readily admit that I am a poor manager. Entrepreneur, know thyself!

I have always preferred to invest the absolute minimum amount of necessary time in matters where I know that I am not a shining light. Our time is limited, so it is best used to develop the skills and talents in which we can truly shine. Not just to become good, but to become the best. Even the best in the world, if possible. But this always means that you have to make choices and to specialize.

The business world is finally coming to understand this. In the past, as an entrepreneur, you had to compete with other local entrepreneurs from your own town or region. Nowadays, you are competing with other entrepreneurs from all over the world. Only your best will be good enough.

This is only possible if you focus. Choose the thing that you are best at and go for it two hundred percent. If you need to collaborate with others, pick the companies that are also the best in their field of expertise. This is the only way to truly become a top entrepreneur at world level. But you will never get there if you continue to put your energy into things where you can never become number one.

12 Hunters and farmers

A good salesman is worth his weight in gold. With my sales people, I always make a distinction between 'farmers' and 'hunters'. The farmers work the land; they look after existing customers and seek to get the best possible regular return out of them. Hunters go in search of new customers. You need them both, but the hunters are not always easy to find.

Hunters are hard-nosed individuals who have no qualms about phoning unknown prospects out of the blue. They know that they are often going to be told to 'get lost', but they don't mind banging their head against a brick wall until the successes finally come. If they get knocked down, they immediately spring back up again. This requires plenty of guts and determination. As a result, these special characters are becoming increasingly rare.

For this reason, many companies now try to generate their sales via agents and distributers. In my experience, this approach does not work. Certainly not in the early days of your company's existence. The only way to hear the unadulterated truth about what your customers think of your products is to have your own fulltime sales staff. In this way, the feedback quickly finds its way to the right people. In this early phase, your sales teams are your most important satellites.

At the same time, it is also important to have a direct line between your sales people and the teams that develop and produce the products. This will allow the sellers to know and understand precisely what they are selling.

People who feel closely involved with the company in this way will always be ready to do that little bit extra – to go the extra mile – to win new customers or to keep existing ones. Distributers and agents do not have the same level of connectivity and commitment.

Even so, it bears repeating: sales people are special characters. And special characters need a special approach. I have learned that you need to be careful with sellers who tell you that they are unable to sell a product because it is not good enough or even downright bad. Is the problem really with the product? Or is the problem the way the sales person is trying to sell it?

How to find out? As a test, in one of the companies in which I am active we decided to increase the commission rate from twenty to fifty percent. Surprise, surprise! Sales of the supposedly 'defective' product miraculously shot through the roof! So make sure that you don't act too hastily to revamp your product, just because your sales people say it is no good. First see if you can perhaps give the sales process a boost.

Don't forget to couple the date for the payment of commission with the payment of the invoices to which the commission relates. In the early days at Clear2Pay we made the mistake of paying the commission the moment when the sales contract was signed. As a result, the sales people no longer felt responsible for the customer as soon as they had managed to hook him or her. For them, this particular hunt was over and they moved on to find their next prey. But for a young company a signed contract is just a piece of paper. What you really need is money. For this reason, we decided to defer the payment of sales commission until the customer had settled all his outstanding invoices. In this way, we could be certain that the sales people would continue to work their socks off until every last eurocent owed to us had been received.

But there was something more. We noticed that it was not only the payment of the invoice that caused problems once the contract had been signed. There were also an increasing number of discussions and disputes about the terms of the contracts.

Sales people want to land customers. That is their raison d'être. If they can achieve this goal more quickly and more easily by being 'flexible' with the conditions of the contract in the customer's favor, they are often happy to do so. Of course, this inevitably leads to friction with the company's legal team. Lawyers are trained to assess risks and to provide the best possible defense against them. For the sales teams, the legal department represents 'the dark side'. For the lawyers, the sales staff are unscrupulous money-grabbers, obsessed by their commission.

To resolve this internal conflict, we set up a sandbox. This was a document with certain legal and contractual agreements that the sales teams were obliged to respect. If they operated within the provisions of the sandbox, they were free to draw up their contracts with our customers as they saw fit. But if they wanted to go beyond the provisions of the sandbox, they first needed the prior approval of the CEO or CFO. This usually related to matters such the maximum amount for legal liability, intellectual property rights, and the maximum level of discount.

This 'sandbox' document was the first company document that all our new sales recruits were given. Everyone in the sales department was required to read, mentally digest, and sign it. In this way, we were not only able to avoid a plethora of contractual provisions that went off in different directions, but we were kept fully in the picture about the customers where, for one reason or another, our 'standard' provisions were not applied.

It is crucial to keep a close watch on your sales teams. But how exactly can you best do this? To start with, you need to define a set of variables that are important for your sellers. I always use the following parameters, especially in technology companies: the sale of licenses, the sale of services, the size of the pipeline, the degree of accuracy, the level of activity, housekeeping, and account management.

The first two variables deal with actual sales during a certain period. With 'accuracy' I mean how accurately the seller can predict potential sales in the pipeline. Will he or she succeed in closing the prospective deal in the quarter he or she predicts? The level of activity measures the number of calls and visits. Housekeeping refers to the quality of the seller's reporting. For example, how much time elapses between contacts with prospects and the processing of the meeting in a tool like Salesforce? Account management relates to the churn percentage of the current customer portfolio: how many customers stay on board and how many jump ship?

In my dealings with sales people I always add a different weighting to each of the seven variables. In particular, these weightings need to be different for hunters and farmers. Both have completely different profiles. For example, a hunter doesn't need to be concerned about account management, whereas for a farmer that is a matter of crucial importance.

Of course, every company is free to set and vary its own percentages. Even so, the following example may be useful:

		Hunter	Farmer
1	License sales	50%	25%
2	Service sales	10%	20%
3	Pipeline	15%	5%
4	Accuracy	9%	9%
5	Activity	11%	8%
6	Housekeeping	5%	8%
7	Account management	0%	25%

On the basis of the points each seller scores for each parameter, adjusted to take account of the relative weighting per parameter, it is possible to draw up a league table for your sales force. Believe me, there is no better motivator than a system of internal comparison. No one wants to be at the bottom of the rankings, and certainly not quarter after quarter.

In addition to their rivalry with their colleagues, there is another factor that drives sales people forward. This will require me to let you in on a secret. True, it is an open secret, so I hope that my sales colleagues won't mind me putting it down in black and white. The secret is this: good sales people are always short of money. Let me explain.

Hunting for new customers is an intense process. It demands energy and per-sistence. Even if you have had ten refusals today, you still need to pick up the phone and call the eleventh prospect on your list. And because it is so difficult and so mentally challenging, sales people need to wind down every now and then. Expensive whisky and exclusive cigars can be an excellent remedy for stress, as is a day at the spa. As a result, good sales people often have a tendency to spend more than they earn. Which means that they need to find lots of new customers to make ends meet and maintain their lifestyle. And so the cycle is perpetuated …

13   The Porsche

I am on the board of directors of a number of companies and I put a lot of time and energy into these different roles. Not only because I like to pass on my knowledge and experience, but also because each of these companies gives me new and different insights, insights that I can then apply in my own companies, faster than would otherwise have been the case.

In my opinion, an entrepreneur should be a director in at least one other company. Agreed, it costs valuable time and time is money. But it helps you to learn about new and different sectors and allows you to extend your network to people that in other circumstances you might never have met. Sooner or later, this is guaranteed to be useful.

One of the companies where I was on the board had a self-confident and head-strong CEO. It was his habit to omit difficult subjects from the formal agendas for our board meetings, preferring to deal with these matters at the last minute under 'any other business'. Trying to rush things through in this manner always sets off an alarm bell inside my head. So I was on my guard when one day the CEO announced that he had a 'brilliant plan'.

The company was finding it difficult to keep its young sales personnel motivated. The company sold software door-to-door with a direct sales model. It was a frustrating job, since it involved hard selling with a low hit ratio. Or to put it in other terms, the young salesmen and women often found the door slammed in their face, mostly figuratively, but sometimes literally. How could the company persuade these young and talented people to put all this rejection to one side and move on to the next door with the same enthusiasm?

According to the CEO, the solution was simple. He proposed that the company should splash out with the purchase of a brand-new Porsche. During the week, he would have use of the car (which he felt was appropriate for his status). During the weekend, it could be used by the sales person who had sold the most software during the past seven days.

The CEO was certain that this would be a fantastic incentive. I thought that it was a stupid idea. In previous board meetings I had been constantly hammering on about the need to keep costs under control and now he was proposing to 'invest' a sizeable amount of our precious resources in a luxury sports car! From the perspective of good housekeeping, it was madness.

For all my sound arguments, I ended up losing the discussion. The CEO was able to convince the majority of the board that the Porsche would soon pay for itself through increased sales. It was agreed that we would try it for six months. If the Porsche hadn't had the desired effect on the sales force by then, it would be sold.

The company in question was later launched on the stock market and grew to become a major success. During the period of due diligence – the negotiations with the banks and potential investors to assess the company's stock market-worthiness before the launch – the same question was raised time after time. Why did the sales graphic show a sudden upwards surge the previous year? What had happened to give the sales such a boost?

The answer was simple. The peak in the sales figures corresponded exactly with the purchase of the Porsche. The CEO had been right. Every member of the sales team had made a superhuman extra effort. They all wanted to drive home in the car on Friday evening! But that was not all: everyone who was fortunate enough to enjoy the car for a weekend was burning with ambition to do it again. And again. And again. Imagine: you are 23-years old and have the opportunity to parade around your home town in one of the flashiest cars on the road. Your friends – especially those who you'd like to be more than just friendly with ... – suddenly think you are mega-cool. Until you have to explain why you haven't got the car the following weekend. As a result, furious but healthy competition developed within the company, which saw everyone do their absolute best to become 'sales employee of the week'.

The Porsche did indeed pay for itself in record time; less than a year, in fact. Even for me, with all my experience up to that point, it was an important new lesson learned. Yes, you need to keep the costs in your company under control. But you need to view those costs in relation to the speed with which they can bring you a return. And that can sometimes happen faster than you think.

14   From serial to parallel

If you google my name or take a look at my LinkedIn profile, you will see that I have lots of different irons in the fire. I have my investment fund, but I am also active in companies in sectors as diverse as construction, retail, technology and health care. People who do not know me personally imagine that I must be like a deranged Duracell Bunny, rushing here, there, and everywhere, but unable to focus for any length of time on one specific key area.

But that is definitely not the case. I have made a very conscious choice to be active in different companies and sectors simultaneously. This kind of parallel working has been a constant theme throughout my professional career; in fact, throughout my whole life. I do not wish to restrict myself to just a single world. Instead, I want to constantly search for new experiences.

This philosophy has helped to make me who I am. What's more, I am convinced that it is a recipe for success. It allows you to develop skills in sector X that you can then employ in sector Y. In this way, you continually combine the best of both worlds, while at the same time ensuring your own further personal growth. Of course, your company benefits as well.

For example, I learned a lot through helping a friend who was a sales manager for a multinational. He was not so good at making the macros he needed to monitor his sales teams properly, so I did it for him. In the process, I quickly discovered how the sales world operates, a world that had previously been a complete mystery to me. Similarly, I once helped another friend in HR to design an evaluation model for her company's employees. It taught me a huge amount about personnel policy and the best way to use evaluation systems to get the most out of people. For a third friend – this time a lawyer – I once translated a take-over contract into English. Result: it focused my attention on the importance of certain clauses in this kind of document and allowed me to be on the lookout for them in the future.

Most people don't like to work in parallel. They often remain in the same sector throughout their career. In fact, they often remain in the same company (although this is less the case with today's younger generations). Of course, they learn new skills as their careers progress, but these are in line with the requirements of their existing job and can only be applied in the same sector. In other words, their development is serial, not parallel.

If you work in parallel from the start of your career, your learning curve will climb much more steeply that someone whose work is organized serially. As an entrepreneur, you don't need to be smarter than everyone else in absolute terms. I am certainly not a genius, but I acquired lots of experience much more quickly than many of those around me. It is experience that allows you to make the difference, not raw intelligence. And the good news is that you can easily acquire that experience for yourself, wherever and whenever you like.

My sixteen-year-old son wanted a computer for his gaming. Apart from a little English and a great deal of manual dexterity, there is not much that gaming can teach you. For this reason, I wanted to encourage him to think parallel. We went to the shop to buy a new computer, but instead of buying a ready-made one I bought him all the component parts to make one himself.

'But dad,' he moaned, 'I know nothing about building computers.' 'Well, then,' I replied, 'now is the time to learn. Perhaps you might need a little help from your friends?' It took him a quite a while, and during the following months I regularly heard him chatting with his pals: 'What is this? How does it work? Where does it go?' In the end, however, he succeeded in piecing together his own computer – but only because he was prepared to step out of his comfort zone.

I also apply this same parallel philosophy in my home life. Thanks to the internet, nowadays we can learn almost everything about almost anything. One day on impulse I bought a whole squid. Not the calamari rings you can buy in packets in the supermarket, but the whole thing, tentacles and all. My wife laughed at me and said I had no idea how to clean and cook my new purchase. Which was true, of course. But all the information I required was already in my back pocket. Ten minutes on my smartphone and a quick look at one of the many 'How to clean, cut, and cook a squid' films on YouTube was all I needed. And the resulting meal was delicious!

There is only one way
to avoid criticism:
do nothing, say nothing,
and be nothing.

– *Aristotle*

15   The chicken syndrome

As everyone who has children will know, there comes a moment when the kids want to (and are allowed to) stay 'home alone' for the very first time. This is a tense moment for parents, because you never quite know in advance exactly what your wannabe grown-ups are planning and how they will cope. Will they hold a party? Annoy the neighbors? Perhaps even burn down the house?

Some time ago, my children were also home alone for the weekend. All I had asked them to do was buy some meat on Saturday, meat that I would then use to cook a pasta dish when I arrived home on Sunday evening.

My only instructions were short and simple (or so I thought): 'Go to the butcher's in the village on Saturday, because he is closed on Sunday, and buy 700 grams of chicken fillets.' That sounds clear enough, doesn't it? There is not much that can be misunderstood, is there? I should have known better.

I was in Morocco when my phone rang on Saturday afternoon. I could see that the incoming call was from my son, which was not his habit, and so I picked up immediately. For a second or two, every conceivable disaster scenario flashed though my mind. 'Sorry, dad,' he said. 'There's a problem with the chicken.' It turned out that he had bought slices of pre-cooked chicken fillet of the kind to put on your sandwiches, rather than the raw chicken fillets I had in mind. Seven hundred grams is an awful lot of slices, and there is not very much you can do with them in combination with pasta!

I could hardly contain my laughter and told him to get back down to the butcher's before he closed. My son found it less amusing, because he was convinced that he had carried out the task I had set him correctly. And, of course, he was right. I had set him a task exclusively from within my own frame of reference. How was he to know that I intended to use the chicken in a pasta dish? All I had said was 'buy 700 grams of chicken fillet' and that is what he had done.

This story has its parallels in entrepreneurship. As an entrepreneur, you will often have an idea in your head that is so clear and so blindingly obvious to you that you assume everyone else must also be able to see it. However, this perception is the result of your own experience, your own environment, and your own frame of reference. Which may not be the experience, environment, and frame of reference of your employees.

As a result, in your company you will probably be confronted quite often with the 'chicken syndrome': you give your people what you think is a crystal-clear task, but the outcome is totally different from what you expected, leading to frustration, not only for you but also for your staff.

There comes a time when every entrepreneur has to delegate. As your company grows, it is impossible to keep on running a one-man show. But even delegation has its problems. You will often think that you don't have sufficient time to explain assignments to your people in detail. Besides, what is the point of delegating if you have to explain everything from A to Z? In that case, you could just as easily do the task yourself!

This is false reasoning. It is important to take all the time you need to explain to your staff what you expect of them and to outline the pitfalls they may encounter along the way. Don't simply assume that they see the world the same way as you do. The time that you spend with them to outline your vision clearly, as it seems to you from within your own frame of reference, will be won back twice over if they then carry out the task efficiently and effectively.

16 Fundraising: how to start

Courtship is the special ritual form of behavior that animals demonstrate before they mate. Each species has its own different form. With color, scents, sounds or movements, they attempt to seduce a partner of the opposite gender. For example, birds of prey display their urgent desire to mate with spectacular feats of aerial aerobatics, while the male giraffe does the same by sniffing and tasting the urine of the female, as a way of checking that she is fertile. To each his own …

People also demonstrate courtship behavior. In my professional sphere, the acquisition of funding has similarities with courting and seduction. It is a game of repeated attraction and rejection, for which there are unwritten rules that must be respected and steps that must be followed. A degree of subtlety is required but your signals must be clear enough to avoid the wrong interpretation of your message. You must be patient and seek to find a happy medium between being too enthusiastic and too hard to get.

In short: fundraising is an art. Fortunately, it is an art that you can learn.

Nowadays, I am primarily active as an investor via SmartFin, the fund that I set up five years ago with my partner, Bart Luyten. With Clear2Pay, and various other companies, I was the one who needed to go in search of funding. But now that entrepreneurs come to me seeking funding, I have sat on both sides of the table and the experience has taught me important lessons.

The first question that you must always ask yourself is this: do you really need venture capital to make your company grow? Many start-ups seem to think that they can only get themselves on the business map if they are able to attract this kind of capital. They see it as a sign to the world that they are now playing with the big boys. But is that actually the case? I'm afraid not. The reality is often very different from the perception. Only sixteen percent of the fastest growing companies in the United States between 1997 and 2007 made use of venture capital. In other words, it is perfectly possible for a company to grow both large and fast without hauling a venture capitalist on board.

But what if you remain convinced that your company needs an injection of external cash to realize its dreams? Be aware that of every hundred pitches that are made only ten are investigated in detail. And at the end of the road, only one of these ten actually wins the jackpot.

Put simply, the vast majority of companies do not come into consideration for the awarding of venture capital and they never will. They are in the wrong industry, or don't have the right team, or simply lack the potential to make them interesting for a venture capitalist.

Once you have decided that you need funding, the second key question you need to ask is whether your company and its activities will make it possible for the gross margin to grow as a percentage of revenue. True, a company can still be a very interesting prospect even if the gross margin is unlikely to grow into a larger percentage of revenue, but in that case the business model is generally not attractive for investors and they will probably not be willing to put money into your company.

In today's economy, companies with growing gross margins are found, for example, in the software and biotechnology industries. In the former, you need to invest heavily to build the initial software; in the latter, you need to invest heavily to secure the all-important approval of the FDA. But once you have overcome these obstacles, the cost of each extra product that you sell is marginal. This means that you can scale up quickly, allowing your gross margin to soar. Whether a thousand or a hundred thousand customers use your software makes no difference. With each new customer, your gross margin increases.

In contrast, the gross margin in other sectors – say, the world of consultancy – remains relatively constant. Customers pay for each hour of performance. You can increase your hourly rate, but there is a limit to what you can get away with in that respect. If you really want to increase your revenue, you will need to recruit more consultants. But you will also have to pay them. In other words, your revenue will increase, but so will your costs. Once again, this is less attractive for potential investors, because a gross margin of ninety percent or more – margins that are achievable in the software and biotech industries – are not feasible in consultancy over a long period.

Nine months of preparation

Many start-ups and scale-ups underestimate how much time is necessary to secure venture capital. A rough estimate? For a period of six to nine months, the process will take up sixty percent of the CEO's time, sixty percent of the CFO's time and forty percent of the CTO's time.

And while all this is going on, the sales figures need to remain on track, the finances need to remain in balance, and the right people need to be recruited and persuaded to stay. Put simply, you need someone to run the shop while the company's top brass is attempting to secure the money needed to make that shop grow.

I have often seen companies invest so much time in trying to gain additional funding that they start to miss their basic targets. The quest for extra cash pushes all their other activities into the background. As a result, the entrepreneurs in question have to accept a too low valuation of their company. While they are sitting around the table with potential investors, the latter can watch almost literally from the front row how the company's monthly figures take a downward turn.

If the company had not put all its eggs in the single investment basket and instead continued to focus equally on its core business, it would have been possible to conclude a much better deal with the money men.

So is someone looking after your shop? They are? Okay, then you can begin with your fundraising. Good preparation is crucial. Here are a few tips that you may find useful; tips that I learned the hard way:

- In most of the companies where I am active, I set up three different committees right from the very start: an audit committee, a remuneration committee and an exit committee.
  The remuneration committee is responsible for everything connected with salaries, bonuses, stock options, etc. It checks to see if the company's level of remuneration is in line with the market and makes use of relevant benchmarks. At the same time, it monitors the decisions of management relating to promotions and career planning.

The audit committee has the 'pleasant' task of monitoring everything relating to the financial aspects of the company. This is mega-boring, but oh so important! Perhaps for this reason, it is my favorite committee.

Later in the book, in the chapter on M&A, I will explain the importance of having an exit committee in more detail. Many starter entrepreneurs fail to see the need for this committee, which is only logical: you have only just set up your company; why should you already be thinking about a possible exit? You have masses of work and you want to grow still further. At this stage, selling should be the last thing on your mind, shouldn't it?

- Just as many companies fail to see the need for an exit committee, so many others are just as firmly convinced (incorrectly) that they need the services of an investment banker. Let me be crystal clear on this point: to organize the fundraising process, you do not – I repeat, not – need an investment banker. As the founder of your company, you know much more about it and about your sector than anyone else, and certainly more than an investment banker. Why pay someone a fee of between four and seven percent of the acquired capital when it is not really necessary? It is money down the drain.

- It is important to involve your existing shareholders in the fundraising process right from the very beginning. Ask them in advance what conditions they will be willing to accept for venture capital financing. Draw up these conditions into a formal document and have them sign it. In this way, you can avoid the need to constantly go back and forth between your shareholders and your potential investors. All that to-ing and fro-ing not only costs a lot of time, but also creates a poor professional impression and undermines your authority in the eyes of your investment partners. They want to discuss things with someone who is able to make the necessary decisions.
Even so, make sure that you always know where your shareholders are likely to be at crucial moments. Nothing is quite as frustrating or stressful as having to chase around for the signature of that last shareholder, who has just jetted off to some exotic island in the Caribbean!

- Media attention can give your fundraising efforts a serious push in the back. In the run-up to or during your discussions with the venture capitalists, it can never do you any harm to get the name of your company in the papers or on TV. This helps you to create the necessary buzz and credibility. The investment world is small; everyone knows everyone else. If you can make yourself the 'talk of the town' in that world, this will not only increase interest in your company but perhaps also its valuation. On the reverse side of the coin, unknown is very often unloved – as you will read in a later chapter.

- Timing is everything. Getting off to a good and early start is crucial. It is better to seek additional funding at a time when you don't (yet) need it. If you start looking for funding when your bank balance is already in the red, your investors will see this for what it is: a clear sign of weakness. They will either back out or else they will take advantage of the situation to make extra demands or reduce the valuation.

- Only talk with the partners of the investment fund. If you suddenly get a mail or a telephone call from an 'interested' investor, this might give a nice boost to your ego, but that is all it will do. Nine times out of ten it is a junior staffer who makes the call or sends the mail, purely to collect as much information as possible about a particular sector. It may seem a bit arrogant, but tell them that you don't have time to waste on this kind of questioning. If your company is really interesting, a partner will make the effort to contact you personally.

- Is it okay for you to make contact directly with a potential investor? Of course it is! They are not inaccessible rock stars; they are people like any other. But is it wise to contact them in this way? Not always. You will have more chance of success if you can find someone who has the ear and the confidence of the potential investor to make a first introduction. In this way, the introduction will serve as a kind of quality label.

- It is not necessary to draw up a full-scale business plan. This is just a waste of energy. A good investor gets dozens of plans sent to him or her each week and simply doesn't have the time to read them all in detail. In this sense, you can compare investors with publishers: they never read the entirety of the manuscripts they are sent, but dip into them here and there to assess the potential of the writers. And that is how it is for start-ups and scale-ups that go knocking at the door of the venture capitalists. I hate to break it to you, but if I receive a lengthy business plan as part of an investment proposal, there is a very strong likelihood that I will never read it. In fact, if there is no summary, there is an even better chance that it will end up in the waste paper basket!

- So what should you do? Limit the presentation of your company to just ten slides. Investors don't like looking at long presentations. Research suggests that 3 minutes and 44 seconds is the average. Investors are most interested in your team and your finances, so devote the most time to those subjects. But there is no point in drawing up a financial plan for the next three years. In our rapidly changing modern world, three years is an eternity. Despite the claims of certain gurus to the contrary, no one can predict what is going to happen in the next three months, never mind the next three years. So don't believe them.

- An analytical profit and loss account and an accurate summary of the cash flow situation are much better indicators than a three-year plan. Most long-term plans have no decent cash flow planning or else only calculate them on an annual basis. This is not enough: only a monthly cash flow summary can provide the necessary insights. Be certain to also make a distinction between operational cash flow, investment cash flow, and financial cash flow. Many entrepreneurs and even CFOs have problems estimating cash flow accurately. In Europe in particular, this is an aspect of the business world where there is still major room for improvement.

- One of the things that has always helped me immensely is the Excel spreadsheet that I always use to simulate the EBIT and cash flow figures. This is the spreadsheet I talked about in the fifth lesson: 'Slower. Less. Costlier.' It actually sounds more complicated than it is. With this spreadsheet you can simulate in real time every possible scenario that the investor is likely to suggest. If he asks what the effect will be of lower income, you can tell him almost immediately: 'If my income drops by ten percent, then …' The ability to give reliable and realistic answers to this kind of question sends a hugely powerful signal.

- The opposite is also true: a CEO who doesn't know his figures sends out a weak signal. Learn by heart as much as you can about the finances of your company. I am always disappointed when I see a CEO turn desperately to his CFO to help him deal with a question that he should have been able to answer himself. If you don't know what percentage of expenditure goes on R&D or what last year's EBIT figure was, then you are not much of a CEO!

- Finally, make sure you practice your pitch. A lot. The best speeches have often been rehearsed over and over again. Someone like Barack Obama was able to create the impression that his speeches were 'spur of the moment', but that was seldom the case. He came across as being natural and super-relaxed because he knew every comma and full stop in the text. In short, he was in full control. And that is the way you need to be with your investment pitch. Practice makes perfect. So practice in front of a mirror and practice with your family and friends. Remember that even your mother-in-law needs to understand what you are saying and must be able to pick out the salient points of your proposal.

You can always add an appendix to your presentation, with a dozen or so nerdy slides and graphics that you can 'magically' bring up if anyone asks more in-depth questions. But your ten basic slides must be crystal-clear. The ideal pitch should convince your investors that they need you – and not the other way around.

17   Fundraising: pitching, negotiating and closing the deal

So far, so good. You have attracted the attention of the investors and you have been given an appointment to make a pitch for your company. Now is when the hard work really starts. You need to convert that theoretical interest into hard investment. From this point on, most entrepreneurs find themselves sailing in uncharted waters. They are entering a new world which can seem both complex and intimidating.

For this reason, it is important to find the right expert to help you. Your friendly neighborhood lawyer will no doubt find it cool if you ask him to help negotiate your investment deal. But there is too much at stake to be swayed by ties of friendship. If you want to give your tame lawyer a unique experience, buy him a Sudoku Rubik's Cube instead. For your fundraising, you really need someone who knows what he or she is doing. In short, a specialist.

I still meet entrepreneurs who are convinced that they can negotiate and draw up the funding contract themselves. This is a very dangerous idea. In contracts with investors, a single word can make a world of difference. A seemingly unimportant detail can come back years later to hit you in the face like a boomerang. Hiring some expertise in this kind of situation is not a luxury; it is a necessity.

The pitch

If your pitch is ready and you have practiced it so that you now know it backwards, forwards and sideways, the time has come to test it in front of a live audience. After all, actors and stand-up comedians also try out their material before they go on tour. For this purpose, it is a good idea to try and find a small group of venture capitalists from whom you do not want money. Don't tell them, of course, that you are using them as guinea pigs, but carefully note their answers, reactions and feedback. This will help you to modify your pitch for the investors who really matter. In this way, your pitch will evolve constantly. It is dynamic, a living thing. By the time you make it for real, it will have been honed to perfection and you, as its presenter, will be razor-sharp.

Testing out your pitch will also help you to make it with conviction. Investors want to hear a story. They are not interested in entrepreneurs who simply read off a set of slides. If need be, they can read the slides themselves! Storytelling – creating a narrative – is therefore very important. Say where you got your idea; where your drive to solve problems comes from (perhaps as a result of a personal frustration or experience); what obstacles you have met so far and overcome; where and how you found the members of your team. Spice up the story with relevant anecdotes.

Investors meet a lot of entrepreneurs. You need to grab them by the scruff of their necks, give them goose bumps. They want to see authenticity and passion. It goes without saying that not every entrepreneur is a 'natural' on a podium, but even if you possess charisma by the bucketful you are not guaranteed to be a success. And the reverse is also true: modesty can also engender confidence and trust. Even Mr. Nondescript can turn out to be a top entrepreneur!

But whatever your character, whether you are a mouse or a lion, you need the right powers of persuasion. If you have lost the attention of your investors after the first two minutes, they won't bother looking at your figures. And then they may never find out just how impressive those figures really are.

I am a great advocate of making the pitch as a team. That being said, sending a team as a substitute for your CEO is simply not done. 'Sorry, but our CEO had another urgent appointment with a customer' is the worst excuse of all time! Nine out of every ten investors will immediately show you the door. If the CEO doesn't think the fundraising is important enough to make the necessary time to attend, the investors will think that they also have better things to do with their own valuable time – and money. What if you know, as a CEO, that you are not the world's best pitcher? Play to the strengths of your team, but make sure that you are there to watch them do it.

Often companies send only a relatively limited team to make the initial pitch. 'We'll send a bigger delegation next time,' they say. This is not the kind of approach calculated to fill investors with confidence. Of course, you can expand the size of your team as the company grows. But investors want the guarantee that the company already has the necessary clout to make good its promises and ambitions.

For this reason, it is better to send a strong team to argue your case. This may cost more, but it is an investment that will pay for itself if the fundraising is successful. Also, make sure your team includes as few part-time members as possible. And definitely no consultants. Investors want to see the sparks of your own enthusiasm flying through the meeting room. They need to be sure that everyone in the company is two hundred percent behind the pitch.

Start your pitch by introducing your team and give them all the opportunity to say a few words. A pitch where the CEO monopolizes all the talking and tries to steal the show from the other members of the team will never be well received. It gives the impression that the CEO regards himself or herself as more important than both the team and the company.

If everyone is going to speak, it is important to agree clearly in advance who will say what. And not just for the pitch: also decide who will answer which questions in the Q&A session. Of course, it is always possible that you will be thrown an unexpected question, but the majority are fairly easy to predict – especially after you have had a few try-outs.

Remember to get your story straight. I have been at some pitches where the various team members have actually contradicted each other. There are differences of opinion in any company, but during a meeting with your potential investors is not a good time to air them. Honest as it might be, it comes across as confusing and unprofessional, while seriously undermining the authority of the CEO.

An investment pitch is too important to leave anything to chance. For this reason, I am not in favor of including live demos in pitches. There is too much that can go wrong. At best, you will be wasting the valuable time the investors have given you; at worst, it will turn into a complete shambles. If you can't make your product work during a crucial meeting, why should investors have confidence that it will perform perfectly out in the real world?

But if you firmly believe that a live demo is vital to your chances, then you must test and re-test all the connections and technical aspects in advance. Make sure all the cables are plugged in and that you know the WiFi codeword without having to ask someone when you are ready to start.

Fifteen percent of fundraisings are completed within five weeks. Roughly half take between eleven and fifteen weeks to complete, while seventeen percent take sixteen weeks or longer. This means that it is important to remain in close contact with the potential investor after the pitch has been made. The key to success in this period is making your voice heard, but without seeming to be desperate or pushy. Continue to do your homework and be ready to provide any additional information that is necessary, within the broad parameters of your pitch. However, if you are dealing with venture capitalists, it is not acceptable to change the timing and/or the amount of your fundraising request en cours de route.

Last but not least, the question that every interested reader has probably been waiting for: how do you decide how much your company is worth? The short answer is that you don't. You need to leave this valuation to the investors. It is not a good idea to put forward your own figure. The venture capitalists will try to make you commit yourself, but you must resist: immediately play the ball back over the net, by telling them that you expect the valuation to be in line with what the market generally pays for a company of your type.

Don't allow yourself to be blinded by the valuation. You must always view it in relation to the associated contractual provisions. The valuation and the provisions form a single whole. You are not going to benefit from a high initial valuation if a whole battery of legal stipulations means that you will be left with significantly less cash after any subsequent exit.

I have never given exclusivity to investors for a fundraising, nor have I ever asked for it. If you are selling your house, it would be madness only to allow visits from just a single potential buyer. This is definitely not the best way to get the best deal. And the same is true for companies and investors.

If you give exclusivity, you fundamentally alter the nature of your relationship with your investor, encouraging him or her to set conditions that are not standard. As long as another investor is still in the running, the tendency to try and impose extravagant conditions of this kind will be significantly reduced. In other words, from the very start of your fundraising process it makes sense to negotiate with at least two venture capitalists – and make sure that they both know it. For example, you can plan consecutive meetings, so that they see each other in the foyer of your office or in the elevator.

I once even organized an event where it was the investors who had to make their pitch to a jury of start-ups and scale-ups. The world turned upside down, you might say. It was interesting to see just how bad the pitches of the professionals could sometimes be!

Just as investors have no qualms about giving start-ups a proper grilling about their plans, so too the start-ups should have no compunction about critically assessing the qualities of the different investors available to them. It never pays to 'jump into bed' with the first investor who comes along. It is much smarter to play the field.

In this respect, it is an interesting exercise to reverse the roles. I would recommend to every start-up that they draw up a list of questions for their potential investors. They are expecting you to sell your company to them; it is only fair that they should have to sell their services to you. Here are some ideas for questions:

- What is the most important reason why you want to invest in my company?
- What are your main concerns about making this investment?
- What are your expectations of our partnership in the coming six to twelve months?
- How will you help us to reach our objectives? What concrete actions will you take?
- How do you see your relationship with our board of directors and what role do you expect to play in this respect?
- What is your scenario for helping companies in the event of a crisis (either internal or external)?
- How have you been able to help companies during the COVID-19 pandemic?
- What was the best and the worst deal of your investment career so far?

If investors fail to answer your questions or answer them badly, you can scrap them from your list. It is true that investors take a financial risk by offering to pump money into your company. But, as an entrepreneur, there is a lot at stake for you as well. The long-term future of your company is too important to conclude a deal with an investor in whom you have anything less than absolute confidence. So dare to be critical!

The deal

When you finally close the deal with the investor and sign on the dotted line of the contract, there are a few possible pitfalls of which you need to be aware.

- Investors often encourage companies to start spending before everything is signed and sealed. If they are not careful, these companies can burn up their money reserves and soon find themselves in cash flow difficulties, as a result of which they may be forced into accepting poorer terms and a lower valuation as the only way to correct this precarious situation. So if an investor says to you 'Go ahead, spend all you like,' never take any positive action until the agreed investment amount has been credited to your bank account.

- Always avoid partial financing on the basis of milestones. Partial financing leads to partial expenditure. This makes it harder to reach the objectives you have set. If a venture capitalist suggests funding your company in several phases, you should show him the door. Immediately. Payment in phases is often suggested with the intention of renegotiating the price for the second and each subsequent phase, if you fail to reach an agreed milestone. In other words, they are deliberately attempting to complicate your work in the hope of being able to get a better price in the long run. Make sure you don't fall for this trick.

- A golden tip for any deal: ask for a share option plan of ten percent and ensure that this is a permanent right. If you later raise new capital or need to finance a takeover, as a result of which that original ten percent is watered down, you can always create new options of up to ten percent. Moreover, share option plans make it possible to avoid a situation whereby in the long run you no longer have any real interest or stake in the company that you single-handedly created from nothing. Fortunately, there are also other ways to avoid this, which we will look at more deeply in the chapter 'Show me the money'.

- In my role as an entrepreneur, I have always avoided complex legal structures. If you make concessions to an investor in a contract, you will never be free of them. In any following rounds of fundraising, the new investor will ask as a minimum for the same rights and conditions as the previous investor. In other words, the fewer rights you concede to your initial investors, the stronger your position will be in the long run.

- Always draw up a detailed term sheet when negotiating with an investor. This will make it much easier when you later need to draw up new legal documents relating to the funding, since many of the relevant matters will already have been dealt with in the term sheet. If your term sheet is insufficiently detailed or if certain key definitions are omitted, you will find it much harder to insist on correcting these oversights during the drafting of the final contracts.

18 After the fundraising

Always make sure you know who will represent the venture capitalist on your company's board of directors. The best person is probably the investment manager who conducted the funding deal on behalf of the capitalist. If the venture capitalist attempts to saddle you with one of his old associates – someone for whom he needs to find a job or wants to do a favor – you should try to avoid this at all costs. These people often have little feeling for your company or sector.

Let the venture capitalist and his or her people work for your company. Venture capitalists often have a small army of bright young juniors at their disposal who do nothing else but make analyses. Ask them, for example, to make a complete competition analysis for your company or to do detailed market research for the sector in which you operate.

Investors love figures and graphics, and usually assess the development of your company analytically. Make sure that you provide them with new figures each month and, as the CEO, also provide them with a written monthly report. What deals have been signed? Who has been hired and fired? Where are things going well? Where are things going less well?

Always be as honest as possible with your venture capitalist. If there is bad news, don't try to cover it up or gloss over the facts. Tell it like it is and, if necessary, ask for help to put things right.

Also write your reports and minutes in English, so that these can easily be consulted later in the event of due diligence. Make a list with numbered actions for each meeting of the board of directors, which can then be checked number by number at the start of the following meeting, to see if the necessary action has been taken as agreed.

Telephone your investors before each new meeting of the board and discuss any difficult points on the agenda with them in advance. Make sure that you have the support of enough board members before the meeting starts. Always distribute your board pack to each director at least five days before the meeting is scheduled to take place. Many 'hands-on' entrepreneurs often say that they don't have time to do all this paperwork, so they only send out key information to their board colleagues on the evening before the meeting. This leaves far too little time for the information to be read and digested, often leading to poor quality discussion and ill-considered decisions the next day. The evening before the meeting is probably best spent around a dining table with your fellow directors, so that any potential difficulties can be ironed out before (rather than during) the meeting proper.

In conclusion, I would like to give you one final piece of useful advice: remember that a relationship with a venture capitalist is likely to be a long one and that life is too short to be constantly at 'daggers drawn'. So do your best to try and get along with each other.

It's far better to buy
a wonderful company
at a fair price than
a fair company at a
wonderful price.

– *Warren Buffett*

19 Convincing investors in ten slides

A successful pitch is short and to the point. The presentation needs to move at pace, without losing its clarity. Long-winded and complex discourses are a real turn-off for most potential investors, who will generally stop listening after the first few minutes. The perfect pitch deck consists of just ten slides.

1 People invest in other people. There needs to be a connection and a click at the human level. For this reason, I always begin by introducing my team. What did they study? What experience do they have? How long have they worked for the company? Don't forget to mention where they come from and whether or not they have worked together in the past.

2 The second slide should give a helicopter description of the company. You zoom in from a height of ten thousand meters, providing your potential investors with the key facts and figures. In which market is your company active? What are the current financial results? How much new investment do you need?

3 The third slide is crucial and many entrepreneurs wait far too long to show it. This is where you describe the core of the matter: the problem that your company hopes to solve. How big is this problem? For whom is it a problem? What impact does it have on people's lives? To assess these things, you will need to have spoken to enough of your customers beforehand. This is the slide where you now hope to shake your potential investors awake and grab them by the scruff of the neck. Make it crystal clear to them that there is a genuine problem – perhaps a problem that they have not thought about previously – and that a solution is urgently needed. It is only when you have convinced them of this point that they will be willing to listen to the solution you propose.

4 Slide four is where you outline this solution. You don't just explain how you intend to solve the problem, but also why your solution is the right, best, and only solution. Make sure that you don't get too technical. The nuts and bolts of the technical feasibility is something that only needs to be dealt with later on, during the due diligence phase.

5   After the solution comes the market. How big is it? Is it national? International? Are certain segments particularly important? What are the prospects for growth? You might be able to solve a problem, but the market needs to be big enough to allow upscaling and growth.

6   The sixth slide looks more deeply at the likely competition. Who are your most important competitors? What do they do differently from you? What is their market share? Where is the gap in the market that your rivals have failed to fill? If you have a patent, that is certainly something you should mention on this slide.

7   Investors will want to know if your product has traction. Do you already have customers? How well do you know them? How loyal are they? How long is the sales cycle? Have you already amended your product on the basis of customer feedback?

8   Of course, you need to explain to the investors precisely how you will earn money with your solution. Slide eight therefore highlights your business model and your financial model. Show key figures but limit yourself to the forthcoming three years. Provide a summary of cash flow for the same period. A full balance sheet is not necessary; figures for the profit and loss account will suffice.

9   Not surprisingly, the investors also want to know how you intend to use their money, if they give it to you. They are not offering a blank check. As a result, this penultimate slide must explain what is known as the 'use of proceeds'. What proportion of the investors' funding will be used to recruit new people; to finance start-up losses; in research; in internationalization; in offices and infrastructure; in production. Just give the headlines; there is no need to go beyond the decimal point.

10 On this final slide you need to look more closely at the current status of the fundraising process and outline the following steps. How far have you progressed in the process and when do you hope to round things off?

You can always make more slides and keep them in reserve, just in case one of the potential investors asks more specific questions. However, my standard deck always consists of ten slides. No more and no less.

Are you putting together your own presentation? Remember that the visual aspect is also important. Devote sufficient care to the layout, form and color. Your slides need to look good and attract attention. Don't fill them with text. Make sure that the graphics are legible and have a title. Of course, ultimately it is the content that counts, but it only requires a little extra effort to make sure that your slides flow. This can only strengthen your story, not weaken it.

Hiring a graphic designer to work on your slides is an investment that will pay itself back many times over. After all, you never get a second chance to make a first impression.

20 Why?

As the founder or CEO of the company, you are often 'the last (wo)man standing'. You have the final responsibility for all strategic, financial and operational matters. Your staff and colleagues bombard you with questions. Certainly, in a young company, it is logical that your people do not follow the hierarchical ladder (often because there isn't one). If they have problems, if they don't understand, if they are losing their way or need confirmation of a decision, they all turn to you. There is always someone tugging at your sleeve, every moment of the day.

You can't just turn these people away. You need to take their concerns seriously, but at the same time you need to find a way to deal with their hundreds of questions efficiently.

Over the years, I developed a highly effective solution. To every question I was asked, I immediately replied with a simple question in return: 'Why are you asking me that?' When I started doing it, a lot of people didn't have a clear answer. They were surprised and hadn't thought about the reasons behind their question. But after a while I gradually began to achieve my objective: getting everyone to think carefully and prepare the ground before they came to me with a query or problem.

A lot of the questions I received in the past were about investment. Investment in new servers, in more staff, in better tools ... My 'why' question ensured that my managers analyzed the situation in advance, so that they could justify their investment request. They came to me with figures to show how the investment would eventually pay for itself over time.

When it came to questions about more staff, this preparation was by no means an unnecessary luxury. When managers are given a budget, they automatically assume that this budget will increase the following year. And if the budget increases, they reason that the number of staff should also increase. And the more staff they have under their control, the more influence and power they will have in the company. Before you know it, you arrive in a situation where the stakes are constantly being raised, but where no one stops to ask whether the extra budget and more staff are actually necessary.

My simple 'why?' always got me a well-justified and substantiated answer. But even more important in my eyes was the fact that my idea of answering a question with a question gradually changed the company culture as a whole. Managers were more careful when it came to extra expenditure and at all levels there was a reflex to measure, to calculate and to formulate concrete KPIS (Key Performance Indicators).

What's more, I not only asked all my people to explain their 'why' on paper, but also made them sign the finished document. In this way, we could see later on who had made a particular decision and were able to assess the assumptions on which it had been based. As a result, no one was able to escape their responsibility for having made a poor decision by blaming an ex-colleague who was no longer there to defend himself. This led to a culture that was efficient, economical and responsible, which is essential for any modern company in today's ultra-competitive world.

21 The bar, the beating heart of every office

There is one key element that all the companies I have ever set up have in common: they all have an office bar. In some of the offices this bar is so prominent that people coming for job interviews think that they have walked into a pub by mistake! We have received more than one telephone call from a confused candidate who feared that he or she had been sent to the wrong address! In Belgium it is almost de rigueur to have a bar that serves alcohol, but you need to be aware that social customs vary considerably from country to country, so be careful before you pop the champagne cork!

The bar is much more than just a fun gimmick. It is the beating heart of every office. On Friday afternoon the week is rounded off with a beer or two (we always have different brews on tap) or a glass of wine. People from different departments meet each other and the distance between them is broken down. Bones of contention are discussed informally and are resolved far more quickly than in half a dozen formal meetings. This is crucial for any growing company.

The bar idea first came to me in 2009, when Clear2Pay moved to new premises on the outskirts of Brussels. The board of directors decided that we should only work with a reputable construction company, specialized in the building of offices. However, I thought that the plans being passed around in our board meetings were expensive and lacking in inspiration. Surely there had to be a better and cheaper alternative?

By chance, I came into contact with Anthony Shaikh and Christophe Erkens, two young architects who had only recently started their own bureau. They had few references to offer but were clearly highly motivated and super-creative. I decided to give them a chance. At our first meeting – for which they arrived on a scooter – I explained my idea for a central hub in the new office. With a bar. In addition, each floor of the building had to reflect one of the different countries where Clear2Pay was active. Open spaces, seats, and (above all) photos and art were also to be given prominence. We all spend more time in the office than at home, so it was important that our people could also feel 'at home' when they were at work.

You can imagine the kind of reaction this got from the board of directors. For the most part, the board members were the representatives of our international investors. In other words, people who were used to a classic corporate office concept. Above all, they were worried by the bar. Wasn't there a risk that we would turn our people into a bunch of alcoholics? To make matters worse, we were planning to collaborate with a small and unknown architectural bureau that no one in Belgium – never mind New York – had ever heard of!

I had to twist a few arms, but the board finally agreed that the two young architects could submit a tender. I can still see them arriving by scooter, their plans rolled up in a cardboard tube under one of their arms. It was a surrealistic sight, because we were talking about a contract worth millions. But in the end, creativity always wins. Their design was innovative and inspirational. The sketches of the bar convinced even the most die-hard members of the board. And, quite humorously, the staff who were asked to comment on the plans thought that they were daydreaming.

We took the risk and awarded the contract to Anthony and Christophe. Their design was not only the most creative but was also by far the cheapest. I gave the board the final push they needed by saying that I would take full responsibility for the project.

It was a huge success. Completed on time and within budget. Anyone who has ever had to build anything will know just how seldom this combination (or even just one of them) truly is.

The new office became the visible symbol for Clear2Pay, a kind of multistorey advertising board. Job applicants were sold on the company before they even walked through the door. Many other technology companies came to take a look and copy some of the ideas. In the end, this drove our HR director half around the bend, since he was the one who always had to give the guided tour. Even Apple and Google sent delegations.

The project also gave a huge boost to the career of the two young architects. From then on, the Clear2Pay office was their visiting card, their signal to the architectural world that they had arrived. In just a few years, their ADMOS bureau grew to become a market leader in Europe. Later, the company was sold for tens of millions of euros to Cushman & Wakefield, a world name in office construction. I helped to arrange and monitor the sale, a collaboration that has rewarded me with friends for life.

Further proof, if any were needed, that it often pays to take risks.

22 What you can learn from the Roman Empire

Power and influence are important forces that have an impact on the growth of your company. Who is really the boss? This question plays an important role in the development of your company's structure.

When you operate in just a single geographical region or have just a single product line, this structure will be relatively simple and will almost design itself. Things become more complicated when you are active in more than one region or have more than one product line. And it becomes truly complex when you are faced with a combination of both. What should you do? Concentrate company power in the center? Or devolve it to the different countries? Or to the individual product lines?

Companies often move backwards and forwards between these different models. Every time there is a new CEO, almost the first thing that he or she does is to announce the need for a new structure. A new emperor means new laws.

I compare this with the rise and fall of the Roman Empire. At first, the Romans kept most things under tight control from their base in Rome. But as time passed, the extent of their empire became so great that they were forced to delegate power to the Germanic peoples living on the empire's distant borders. To protect their homeland while still remaining a world power, they actually needed to surrender some of their power.

In the early years of Clear2Pay, our central office in Brussels was the equivalent of ancient Rome. It was the place where all the decisions were made and it worked perfectly. But a series of acquisitions soon meant that we acquired lots of new products in lots of different countries. Running everything centrally from Brussels was no longer feasible.

As a result, the regions and our local managers were given more autonomy and greater decision-making powers. However, we soon realized this was both a hasty and a bad decision. We were growing so quickly that we did not have the time to draw up and agree on clear terms of action for our foreign agents. Consequently, they began to give their own very different interpretations to HR, finance, legal matters, etc. We suddenly found that our company was moving in all kinds of different directions, with no real common thread. In no time at all, small and independent kingdoms began to appear within our Clear2Pay empire, each with its own customs and laws.

In an effort to combine the best of both worlds, we decided to introduce a new matrix structure, in which people reported both to their geographical manager and to the product managers. It was a kind of 'Judgment of Solomon', which aimed to keep everyone happy and irritate no one.

Of course, it failed miserably. No one was happy and everyone was irritated. The conflicts of interest between regional managers and product managers led to total confusion. People were issued with instructions by both managers that were often contradictory. To make matters worse, some employees began to take advantage of this ramshackle structure. If you have two bosses, you can always play one boss off against the other, blaming the rival boss when things go wrong.

As a result, political skill became more important than technical knowledge and we found that reporting and evaluation were taking up an ever-increasing amount of our time. The moment had come to bury the matrix structure.

Next, we decided to introduce a system that we called 'centralized decentralization'. This involved us making, coordinating and imposing central decisions in matters relating to remuneration, bonuses, contractual provisions, IT, R&D and finance. The regions were expected to remain neatly within these central guidelines but had the freedom and autonomy to arrange other matters in accordance with their own thinking and local practice. You can compare it to a football pitch, where they were free to play as they wished, as long as they kept to the overall rules of the game. Where agreements had been made, they had to be honored to the letter. Where no agreements had been made, the regions could do their own thing.

We also decided to give the regions priority over the products, but each region was obliged to sell all the products. They were also given targets for each product. The development of each product was steered centrally, but its further elaboration was entrusted to the region that had most experience with that specific product.

This new structure allowed us to make the most of everyone's strengths and allowed the regions to be involved in the setting of central policy. Our new motto was 'centralized if it must be, decentralized if it can be'. Which, of course, makes perfect sense. At the end of the day, the local managers are always going to understand their market much better than the managers in a headquarters that is often thousands of miles away. You need to give these local managers as much freedom as you can, but not too much. This is a delicate balancing act and it may take you some time – as it did with us – before you master the skill.

23 Change a winning team

There are periods – lots of periods – when I see the people I work with more than I see my own family. I am certain that is the case for many entrepreneurs. For this reason, it is important to think carefully about who you want to start and/or run a business with. Do your personalities click? Is everybody moving in the same direction? Can you trust each other blindly?

There is no ready-made recipe for building a successful team. However, hard personal experience has helped me to identify a few of the key ingredients.

1   Diversity brings added value to any team. When you start your company, this team will usually be small. Its members will often be friends that you made at university or at a previous employer. This has its advantages. If everyone knows everyone else, decisions can be taken quickly. You don't need formal meetings. A quiet chat around the coffee machine or in the office bar is enough. However, the danger of starting and running a company with friends is that you often all have the same background, the same education and the same vision. All engineers, all developers, all financial wizards. In these circumstances, you will probably all approach problems the same way and from within the same frame of reference. So why not add a historian or a psychologist to the mix? Or perhaps even a philosopher? Diversity can enrich any company. Different profiles and different backgrounds stimulate healthy discussion. Different angles of approach to a problem lead to faster and better solutions.

2   Experience, certainly at the beginning, is a huge bonus. As a start-up, your resources will be limited. You need to make every dollar count. This may tempt you to take on new recruits who have less experience, because they are cheaper. But I have learned that it is worth taking a chance on more expensive candidates with the necessary knowledge and background. Someone who is already familiar with your processes and can work with them quickly and efficiently will soon pay for his or her extra cost. In contrast, someone at the bottom of the learning curve will cost you money through their relative slowness and the mistakes they make. I have already said that time is money, and nowhere is this truer than for a start-up, which generally has so little time at its disposal.

3   Make a clear distinction in your company between entrepreneurs and managers. When you first start the company, you will need more entrepreneurial types, who think and act quickly and have the ability to adapt easily to changing circumstances. If you recruit too many managers at this stage, you risk stifling the creativity and inventiveness that is the life blood of every start-up. After a few years, by which time you may have fifty or so employees, you need to adopt a more formal approach. This is when you need managers to provide the necessary structure. Once again, however, timing is everything. Don't formalize the creative chaos too soon, otherwise you will put the brake on your own innovation and growth.

4   Also make a clear distinction between a start-up mentality and a corporate mentality. As the founder of the company, it is important in the beginning – for as long as it remains feasible – that you should interview every potential new member of staff personally, to see if he or she will fit in well with your start-up culture. People who have worked for years in a large company seldom make the switch to a start-up successfully. In a large company you are familiar with clearly defined structures and are responsible for an equally clearly defined set of tasks. You also have other people around you, to whom you can turn for help to reach your objectives. In a start-up, there is usually no one you can turn to – at least, not initially. As a result, you will often find yourself thrown in at the deep end and will be expected to sink or swim. I am not saying that people in large companies do not have this mentality, but frequently they are suffocated by structure and hierarchy.

5   Don't be afraid to change a winning team. Your original team is not necessarily the team that will help your company to grow successfully in the future. Of course, it is not always easy to accept this and act upon it. You have been through a lot with this original team and it seems harsh to let some of them go, just when things are starting to go so well. As a result, replacing your team – even if it is the right thing to do for the company – is always a heavily charged emotional decision. But these are the decisions that every entrepreneur needs to make. This does not mean that you need to dismiss them entirely. For example, you might redeploy them to launch a new subsidiary in a region where you are not yet active and where their experience of starting up a company can best be put to use.

6   Eliminate your own ego. Changing a winning team means that you must also have the courage to question your own role. Are you still the right man or woman in the right place? Starting a company and scaling it up sometimes takes different qualities than running a company with fifty employees. Just because you are the company's founder does not necessarily mean that you will also be its ideal CEO. Perhaps there will come a moment for the company when it is better if you take a step to one side so that you can focus instead on the things at which you truly excel. This, again, is a difficult emotional decision, but it is one that every founder is honor-bound to make if the circumstances dictate it. I have never been the CEO in any of the companies I have founded, and this was a deliberate choice. As already mentioned, I like to work in parallel, operating in different countries and in different worlds, and this is simply not possible as a CEO. Everyone – not just investors and shareholders, but also the employees – rightly expects that their CEO will be one hundred percent committed to the company. If you only have the title of 'founder', nobody cares what you do in addition to your normal job. However, it is important to give the CEO your full trust. Above all, you need to eliminate your own ego and allow him or her to steal the show in 'your' company.

Do. Or do not.
There is no try.

– Yoda

24 Cultural knowledge and a strong liver

Cultural differences play a crucial role in international entrepreneurship. You need to realize that every culture has its own different rules of engagement. To work well with these cultures, it is essential that you not only understand these rules, but also that you respect them and apply them.

As I mentioned in the beginning of this book, I was born, raised, and educated in Belgium. In addition, I have transacted many of my business dealings in Belgium and, quite often, with other Belgians. If you look on a map of the world, you will see that Belgium and the Netherlands are neighboring countries. Indeed, we even speak the same language, and in a good hour you can travel from Antwerp to Rotterdam. Even so, there are important cultural differences that you need to be aware of and take into account if you want to do business with the Dutch as a Belgian entrepreneur.

Take, for example, the matter of leadership style. In Belgium, the boss is the boss. He or she determines the strategy and everyone else follows. Not so in the Netherlands. When I took over a Dutch company some years ago, I gave an opening speech outlining the new strategy I wanted to pursue. Afterwards, I was amazed that my new Dutch employees openly began to discuss the pros and cons of this strategy. Everyone was prepared to argue with and even contradict the boss. That could never happen in Belgium, where people prefer to beat about the bush. Whenever there is a problem, we never say directly what it is, but suggest what it might be. Others are expected to read between the lines of our meaning.

I am now familiar with the Dutch way of doing things, but it was a bit of a shock when one of my Dutch managers first came up to me and said: 'I suppose you know you're talking total crap!' Nowadays, I appreciate this more direct form of communication. There are fewer sensitivities that need to be considered. People immediately go to the heart of the matter and say exactly what they think. Quick, efficient, to the point and unambiguous. It actually comes as something of a relief if you are used to the Belgian way of communicating.

Many international deals are torpedoed not because of the cost or because of some hidden clause in the contract, but because of cultural differences. The way people eat, greet each other, or dress may trigger unintentional breaches of etiquette and/or politeness. What seems like an odd custom to us can sometimes be a centuries-old tradition to others, to which they attach huge importance.

If you want to do business internationally – and if you want to do it successfully – you must be prepared to learn and abide by these unwritten codes of behavior. If you don't, your foreign adventure is more likely to turn into a foreign nightmare.

Having a knowledge of the culture of your business partner is also a sign of respect. If you can begin your negotiations by showing that you have an appreciation of this partner's customs and traditions, you will already have one foot in the door and your chances of success will increase dramatically.

China: patience is a virtue

China is a special country. The people there won't do business with you straight away. You first have to earn their confidence and trust. They attach great importance to long-term, carefully developed personal relations. Yes, this takes time. Yes, this takes energy (and lots of it). But there are no shortcuts. So don't expect to conclude a deal during your very first meeting, because this is never going to happen. If you push too hard too soon, you will fail.

Long meals, for example, are a part of this process; meals often served at revolving tables, where dish after dish is constantly passing in front of you, each one more exotic than the last. Refusing a dish, no matter how politely you do it, is not done. This will be interpreted as a gross insult to your host and his hospitality. So you need to prepare yourself for eating brains and plenty of other 'delicacies'. And drink. Lots and lots of drink. To do business in China you need a liver made of concrete. What's more, your host will often cart you off to distant restaurants, so that there is less office time available to ask inconvenient questions about tedious financial and operational matters.

During negotiation, those on the other side of the table will never let you fully know what they are thinking. Their reputation for inscrutability is well deserved. They will never make the first proposal but wait until you have made the opening move. Their ancient philosophy tells them that patience is a virtue and that time is on their side. And so they wait. And wait. And wait. And then they strike when they think the moment is right. This is the tried and tested strategy of countless Chinese entrepreneurs. What's more, the negotiations are never really at an end, not even when the final version of the contract rolls out of the printer.

Like the Belgians, the Chinese love to equivocate, vacillate, and quibble, so much so that you constantly need to read between the lines of their words. But they take this much further than their Belgian counterparts. It is not just what is said; the way in which it is said is also important. This is something that is very difficult for a foreign entrepreneur to grasp. From an early age, they are taught to listen not only to what is explicitly spoken, but also – and perhaps even more crucially – to what remains unspoken.

The United States: amazing, fantastic and unbelievable

The first time that I presented my product in the US, I was convinced that I was going to close the deal of my life. My product was 'amazing', 'fantastic' and 'unbelievable'. This was going to be my big breakthrough and I could already see the millions of dollars rolling in. At this time, I didn't yet know that an exaggerated, almost child-like enthusiasm for just about everything is part of the American way of life. And so I left the meeting room certain that the orders would soon follow: quickly, easily and in large numbers. But that's not quite the way it went …

Later, I learned that this behavior was typical: Americans will almost always say your product is 'great', but this doesn't necessarily mean they plan to buy it in the near future. If they say your product is 'interesting', this means they think it is rubbish. You need to take everything they say with a pinch of salt. A very large pinch of salt. Literally hundreds of my American business partners have said something like 'Oh, my god, you have to come over and have dinner and meet my wife.' It has never happened. Not once.

That large pinch of salt is also useful when an American entrepreneur comes to pitch an idea. They talk about their start-up as though they have already conquered half of the world, whereas in reality they don't yet have a product that is even half ready for the market. Likewise, if you get a resume in your inbox, your first thought might be that Superman is looking for a new job. Exaggeration of one's attributes is – for some job seekers – a national sport, and 'modesty' is not a word that you will ever find in any candidate's dictionary.

Yet even if it is often exaggerated and superficial, this American enthusiasm can also be tremendously infectious. It is not something entrepreneurs on this side of the Atlantic need to copy in full, but a bit less European modesty and a bit more American bluff and bluster would do us no harm.

As part of this passion for exaggeration, the Americans also love titles. You need to be boundlessly creative if you want to give a sufficiently dignified title to every member of your American senior management team. And if the words 'vice' and 'president' can appear somewhere in these titles, so much the better. American companies seem to have a vice president for just about everything. This fixation on titles can be useful when people want a salary increase but the budget for such is unavailable. Give them an impressive new title and the demand for extra cash is quickly forgotten.

Finally, I have learned that you need to be careful when it comes to telling jokes to Americans (actually this is true in any foreign culture). Politics, religion, and sexual innuendo are subjects you should definitely avoid. After signing a super-deal, I once joked during a town hall meeting: 'It's a great deal, with all the right metrics. It's like a wet dream come true!' Probably not the best joke of all time, but the local HR manager almost had a heart attack!

South Africa: at least there is no jet lag

South Africa was a special experience. Members of the South African bank came to fetch us from the airport and took us directly to the cellar of their main office. This doubled as a wine cellar, with a fine selection of excellent vintages. Two of us had come from Belgium for the meeting and we were each invited to select a bottle, which we duly did. The two of them then did the same. During the light lunch that followed, we each finished our respective bottles. And then the negotiations began.

I have conducted negotiations on three occasions in South Africa and each time the same scenario played out. I am not certain if this approach has anything to do with South African culture (I doubt it), but it sure as hell works. As Belgians, we have the advantage of being in the same time zone as South Africa, so that if we fly there we are at least spared the additional problem of jet lag. But businessmen from America or China have my sympathy. If you have to fly half way around the world and then drink a full bottle of wine, I can't imagine that it does much for the sharpness of your negotiating skills.

India: no such word as 'no'

In India, the society is organized with extreme respect for hierarchy. So too are the companies. As in most cultures, the citizens want to avoid losing face in front of their hierarchical superiors. As a result, they say 'yes' to almost everything. It doesn't really matter what your question is. The answer is always affirmative. 'Can you do this for me?' 'Yes.' 'Is that feasible within that period?' 'Yes.' It is only a few weeks or months later – by which time you are far, far away – that you discover that the promises were just so much hot air.

Of particular note, those from India have the habit of shaking their head (instead of nodding) as a sign that they have understood. In other words, they are not saying 'no', which is how that gesture would normally be interpreted in Europe and America. This is a good example of how cultural habits, if you are not aware of them, can be confusing and lead to misunderstandings that potentially have far-reaching consequences.

The country's caste system is also extremely difficult for a foreigner to understand, but it is something that is impossible to avoid. Promoting a manager from a lower caste is certain to lead to serious problems on the workfloor. To Westerners, this caste-based discrimination seems ultra-conservative in the extreme and borders on the unacceptable. But if you want to do business in India, you have to learn how to see things through Indian eyes. In fact, that is a lesson that applies to every foreign culture.

I regard it as a hugely enriching aspect of my life that I have been fortunate enough to work in many different countries and, in that way, learn about many different cultures. Even if it sometimes costs you valuable time, it is well worth the effort to find out all you can about the country and the culture in which you intend to operate. In fact, I would go even further: it is absolutely essential, if you want your foreign adventure to be a success.

25 Twenty reasons why start-ups fail[2]

What do Henry Ford, Walt Disney, Bill Gates, Steve Jobs and thousands of other successful entrepreneurs all have in common? Before they enjoyed the sweet taste of success, they all first had to swallow the bitter pill of failure. Sometimes failing is a necessary precursor to discovering the golden recipe for fame and fortune. As an entrepreneur, there is nothing wrong with failing, as long as you learn the right lessons from that failure. Or to put it in the words of the world's most famous inventor, Thomas Edison: 'I have not failed. I have just found ten thousand ways that don't work.'

I often read post-mortem analyses of companies that have gone under. This gives me deeper insight into the reasons why companies fail. After a time, you begin to see the same recurring patterns. On the basis of my own experience and my study of start-ups that have gone out of business, I have listed below (in order of importance) twenty of the most common reasons why start-ups fail. Forewarned is forearmed!

1   No demand in the market for your product

You start your company because you are convinced that your product or service will meet a demand in the marketplace. In ideal circumstances, this product or service will be capable of solving a worldwide problem in a manner that is easily upscalable. Often, however, the problem that you hope to solve is not really a problem at all (except for you) or else your product or service doesn't really solve the problem in the way you had hoped. Just because you think there is a market demand does not necessarily mean that this market demand exists.

2   The wrong team

The quality of your team is an important factor in the development of your company. This team must possess all the skills that are necessary to produce a first version of your product or service.

2 The top 20 reasons startups fail. (2019, 6 November). https://www.cbinsights.com/ research/startup-failure-reasons-top/

Unfortunately, too many start-ups are founded by people whose backgrounds are too similar, a danger that I have already warned of in Chapter 23. As a result, they have a powerful combined expertise in just a single domain but lack essential knowledge in other key domains. A team of engineers may be technically brilliant, but will probably know little about sales, finance, marketing, etc.

In addition to a limited range of expertise, the clash of egos is another factor often responsible for the demise of start-ups.

3   A user-unfriendly offer

One of my companies once developed software that could analyze huge amounts of data at high speed. It was an excellent product. The only problem was that the marketing managers to whom we hoped to sell it needed to be software geniuses in order to use it. They were simply unable to get the program to work. Moral: your product can be outstanding, but if it is not user friendly and is too complex for your target group, it will never be a success.

4   No more money

If your start-up can no longer pay its bills, it will soon be 'end of story'. Carefully monitoring your cash flow, since accessing new funds in good time – via a capital increase or lending – is crucial. Some young companies forget that rapid growth can also have an impact on your cash reserves, and they fail to set aside sufficient working capital to finance this growth. Other companies find themselves burdened with too much debt, so that they are unable to pay back the capital and interest on their loans.

5   The competition is stronger

Interesting ideas, products and services also attract the attention of other entrepreneurs. Every company has competitors. You will never be the only supplier in your market. As a result, it is important to be the first (and preferably also the best) with the solution you are offering. There is no need to over-fixate on your rivals, but you should certainly keep a close eye on them.

Many entrepreneurs fail to make sufficient effort to analyze the strengths and weaknesses of their competitors in detail. What do they do differently? What do they do better? What makes your product unique or better in comparison to theirs? Trying to ignore the competition as though it doesn't even exist is guaranteed to end up in your bankruptcy.

6 An incorrect 'cost versus profit' ratio

It is not always simple to price your product correctly. This price needs to be high enough to cover your costs and make a profit, but also low enough to make it attractive to customers. Starter entrepreneurs often have the tendency to ask too little for their product. They lack the confidence to ask for an amount that the added value of their product or service deserves.

I was once involved with a company that sold its software for 280 euros for a life-long license. The company generated a turnover of a few hundred thousand euros, a sum with which they were happy. When I said that the price was much too low, they resisted my attempts to get them to increase it, because they feared that it would drive away their potential customers. After much internal discussion, it was agreed to raise the price to 3,000 euros per year and per application, which was later raised to 12,000 euros. Just a few years later, the same company had a revenue of more than 10 million euros.

7 A poor business model

Many start-ups initially give away their product free of charge. You can certainly do this to gain your first references – after all, that is what I did with Clear2Pay – but this can only be a short-term strategy. After that, you need to think about how your company can be sustainably developed. How are you going to earn your money and how can that model be upscaled over the long term?

8 A market without money

A friend of mine wanted to build what was effectively a variant of Facebook targeted to societies and associations. It would allow them to share, promote and follow each other's activities, as well as collect their membership fees. On the face of it, it was not a bad idea, but I advised him against trying to put it into practice. Why? Because most societies and associations have very little money at their disposal – and certainly not for a platform of that kind, no matter how useful and user-friendly it might be.

Step one of the start-up process is to find a market that needs your product. But that market must also have the money to pay for it. This, for example, is what makes the banking market so interesting. The one thing they don't have a shortage of is cash.

9 Too dependent on subsidies

I never invest in companies that are only able to make their products or offer their services on the back of subsidies. For me, this is an absolute red flag. Being dependent on subsidies means that you are dependent on political decisions, which are often difficult to predict. Such an unreliable position is a poor basis on which to build a company, because you no longer have your destiny in your own hands. If the relevant authority withdraws its subsidies, there is a risk that your business model will collapse like a house of cards.

10 Poor marketing

Particularly online, your sales will eventually reach a ceiling unless you have proper marketing. Another of the companies I invested in was a producer of beauty care products. Initially, the company's growth was more than reasonable, but after a time the growth curve began to taper off. But when the company recruited someone with a strong online marketing background and allocated a sufficient marketing budget, sales began to pick up again in no time.

Many start-ups underestimate the importance of good marketing or (typical for engineers and developers) have little affinity for it as a key element in a business plan. Once again, your product might be super-good, but you are never going to get anywhere if the market doesn't know that you exist.

11 Not listening to your customers

Start-ups make two major mistakes with regard to customers. One: they wait too long before going to the market. They think that they first need to have a 'perfect' product, but that is not the case. Initial products need to be developed on the basis of customer feedback. This leads to problem number two: entrepreneurs are often so convinced of the merits of their product that they fail to listen to what the customer has to say about it. They are blind to constructive comment and criticism. 'The customers just don't understand,' you hear them say. Maybe they don't, but it is the customers who make or break any company. So make sure that you get to the market as fast as you reasonably can and listen to (and act upon) the feedback you receive. Don't be afraid to make adjustments if you hear that your product is too expensive or not user friendly.

To make this possible, it is important to ensure that you have the channels available to encourage customer interaction and to pick up the resultant feedback. In this respect, customer surveys can also be very useful.

12 Too early or too late

How many times have I already said it? Timing is everything. If the market is not yet ready for your revolutionary product, you have a problem. And if the market is already saturated with your kind of product, you have an equal problem. You need to launch your product at just the right moment: not too early and not too late.

Of course, this is much easier said than done. Yet another friend of mine had the bright idea of opening a vegetarian fast-food chain. When he started, fifteen years ago, healthy food and sustainability were much lower on the social agenda than they are today. Through sheer persistence, he eventually managed to make a success of his chain, but he first had to go through a decade of trials and tribulations, simply because he arrived on the market too soon.

13 Leaving the right path

Start-ups mark out the path they intend to follow, but all too often they have a tendency to deviate from that path too quickly and too easily. They want to score quick wins or to please their most important customer by radically altering their basic product or service. This can work for a single customer, but it is no way to build up a generic product that can be sold on a wide scale.

It is true that start-ups need to be flexible, but by being too flexible – by constantly leaving your chosen path – you will inevitably slow down your growth. Make sure that you always have someone in your company who is responsible for monitoring your road map; someone who is strict enough and strong enough to say 'no' when people ask you to deviate from your fundamental strategy.

14 Arguments and noise

Start-ups where the founders are not united in their vision and are continually arguing about the best way forward are doomed to failure. Entrepreneurship is difficult enough as it is, without the added problem of having to cope with internal disputes, which are usually about power, money, and conflicting egos.

It is vital, right from the very start, to make clear agreements on paper, both between the founders and with the shareholders, and to stipulate unambiguously which scenarios will make further collaboration impossible. In this latter eventuality, also specify what will happen with the start-up.

15 A lack of passion

True entrepreneurs are always passionate about their idea. They want to know everything about the sector in which they are active. They dream at night about their company and at every family gathering they bore their relatives with details about the unquestioned merits of their product or service. However, there are too many would-be entrepreneurs who think that the title 'company founder/owner' looks good on their business card or in their LinkedIn profile, but who are not sufficiently interested in their market or their product to 'go the extra mile' that is necessary for success. Without passion, your chances of making the entrepreneurial grade are zero.

16 Wanting to conquer the world too quickly

Technology is increasingly blurring boundaries. As a result, start-ups nowadays need to think internationally from day one. But many founding entrepreneurs underestimate the impact of internationalization and the pressure it places on their existing team. Going international involves many new challenges: operational challenges, cultural challenges, technological challenges, etc. It is simply not possible to copy-paste the approach you use in your domestic market. International markets involve so much more.

It is certainly important to grow internationally and this ambition must be present from the earliest days of your start-up, but you can only begin to take positive steps in that direction when your organization is ready to cope with the extra strain. If you move too soon, you not only risk jeopardizing your international adventure before it has even started, but also seriously damaging your position in your domestic market. This will quickly bring you back to square one – or perhaps even worse.

17 Trapped in the legal carousel

Legal proceedings (and in particular their heavy cost) can cause the downfall of any company, especially a start-up. Large multinationals know that smaller companies cannot match their resources and strength. Consequently, they keep the legal carousel turning until their smaller rivals are forced to throw in the towel for lack of cash.

Another legal drawback is the fact that start-ups are so keen to attract new customers that they are often prepared to accept unlimited liability as the only way to get the deal that they want. If things then go wrong – if, for example, a delivery goes missing – they risk facing damaging claims for compensation that can bring them into financial difficulties. Never – I repeat, never – accept unlimited liability. It may get you a good deal, but you are risking the future of your entire company. And that is much too high a price to pay.

18 The flame dies

Entrepreneurship places a heavy burden on your health, both physical and mental. When things start to go wrong with their business, entrepreneurs often have the tendency to overcompensate by working even harder, sleeping less, exercising less, and eating worse. Sooner or later, this will inevitably take its toll. Burnouts frequently assume epidemic proportions amongst entrepreneurs.

Large companies can cope if their founder falls by the wayside, but start-ups do not have this luxury. If you are an entrepreneur, it is only normal that you work hard – that is part of the job – but make sure you monitor your physical health and your mental resilience regularly. Otherwise when you break down, your start-up will break down as well.

19 The well dries up

In recent years, there has been much more capital in circulation for start-ups. This money was made available not only by investment funds, but also by 'business angels', who wanted to play at being investors. As a result, a lot of investment money found its way to start-ups that actually had a poor business model which was not sustainable without further injections of cash from the investor.

When the market tightens, these companies will immediately find themselves in trouble. They can no longer attract the additional capital they need and, deprived of this lifeline, they slowly bleed to death.

20 Head in the clouds

When there is plenty of capital available on the market, entrepreneurs sometimes do the craziest (and costliest) things. They invest in matters that are anything but essential for a start-up: a big, fancy office, expensive designer furniture, fast cars, etc. Instead of sandwiches for lunch, they dine out at the finest restaurants and to make sure that they get their name in magazines like *Forbes* they boost their marketing budget to astronomical proportions.

Start-ups always need to remember that attracting capital is just a beginning, not an end in itself. It is an important milestone, but nothing more than that. The hard work still needs to be done. So keep your feet on the ground, and not your head in the clouds.

26 Show me the money

A growing company needs cash. Lots of cash. For this reason, start-ups and scale-ups regularly organize new rounds of funding, where investors pump money into the company in return for part of the shares.

Entrepreneurs do this reluctantly. They are afraid of the dilution of their company. With the addition of each new shareholder, the percentage of shares held by the original shareholders decreases. The founders not only fear that in the short term they will have less and less say in their own company, but even fear that in the long run they might end up with almost nothing to show for all their hard work. What do you gain from a successful exit if successive rounds of capital increase mean that you now hold very few shares in the company that you built with your own hands?

In part, this fear is a matter of perception. Holding a low percentage of shares does not necessarily need to be a problem, if the total value of the company continues to rise. One percent of a hundred million dollars is more than ten percent of a million dollars. Besides, there is another scenario, an ideal scenario, which allows you to bring new money into your company and still maintain your strong position within it.

I always negotiated with investors for an option on half of the shares that they were allocated in return for their funding. This option was valid for a period of ten years. In other words, within a period of ten years I could buy back half of their shares at an agreed price: namely, the price they had paid for them, increased with an annual return of twenty percent. This meant that if, as an investor, you invested one million dollars in my company and received ten percent of the total number of shares in return, I still had the right for a full decade to buy back five percent of the company.

But where could I find the necessary cash for this buy-back? If I had enough cash in the first place, there wouldn't have been any need to go in search of new shareholders. The solution was surprisingly simple: I bought the shares back by selling other shares. If your company grows, its value increases. Consequently, the next time that the company organized a new capital round, I sold a part of my shares at a higher price and then used the money I received personally to take up the option to repurchase half of the shares allocated during the previous capital round.

The more the value of your company's shares increases, the fewer personal shares you need to sell to exercise your option. And if that value increases by more than twenty percent per annum, the series of options is actually a very effective anti-dilution mechanism, because you actually retain more than the extra return you need to pay to your shareholder.

You are probably asking yourself why new investors would agree to this kind of option. If a company is later sold for a price that is higher than the value at the moment when he or she invested their money, they are actually losing out on the deal. So why do it? They do it because they don't expect that this 'loss' scenario will ever happen, which is true in the case of most start-ups and scale-ups.

An investor pumps money into ten companies, in the hope that maybe one or two of them will be a bull's-eye. Consequently, he expects to lose his money in the other eight or nine companies. In these circumstances, the option that I negotiated actually helped to spread the risk for the investor. If I exercised the option, he was certain of a good return for at least half of his investment, which he could then reinvest in other companies. For early-stage funding in particular, a high circulation speed is a major advantage. At the same time, the investor also retained fifty percent of the shares, so that he had the best of both worlds.

I applied this mechanism successfully on several occasions, and as a result I still owned a significant part of the company when the time came to sell it. As the founder, you have put lots of blood, sweat, and tears into your company. All this should be worth every bit as much as the money pumped in by outsiders. 'Show me the money' is just as valid a motto for the founder as it is for the investor.

Investors always say that it is better to have a small percentage of a big cake than a big percentage of a small cake. I think that they are wrong. I have always gone for a big piece of a big cake.

27 Trust is good, control is better

As an entrepreneur, you need to trust people. Sadly, however, it is also necessary to retain and exercise a degree of control. Sooner or later, trust without control leads to problems. This is something that I have learned from hard personal experience, having been surprised by the behavior of my managers and associates on more than one occasion.

A code of conduct is indispensible for every company. And everyone in the company – from the cleaning staff to the CEO – needs to be familiar with it. If people do not know what kind of behavior is expected from them, you can hardly blame them or sanction them when they overstep the mark. Clear rules and clear red lines that people must not cross are essential.

In one of the companies where I was active we once had a problem with sensitive information being leaked from the senior management committee, not only to other members of staff but also to outsiders. It was possible that the leak came from a member of the committee, but there were others who had access to the same confidential facts and figures. For example, the secretaries who typed up and distributed the minutes of the committee's meetings. One thing was certain: information was Ieaking from somewhere, deliberately or not.

You can imagine the kinds of scenes and the atmosphere that this generated inside the company. Everyone suspected everyone else. Rumors, suspicions, and false accusations were rife. This can be fatal for any organization.

After a full-scale internal inquiry and an audit, it became clear that the leak was originating from the IT department. The computer operative in question found it 'interesting' to read the emails that circulated between the members of the senior management team. He was not deliberately attempting to damage the company; he just wanted to know what was going on. Unfortunately, he was also an incurable gossip, who could not resist the temptation to pass on the information to his colleagues. But unintentional or not, the damage to the company was nevertheless serious.

This illustrates the importance of having an internal tracking system. Who has access to what information? When and for what reason can the company deviate from these rules? If a leak occurs, you must be able to identify its source with minimum delay. In this way, you can prevent mutual suspicion and distrust from causing deep wounds.

I have also been faced with situations where people leaving the company have copied huge amounts of data before they go, with the intention of passing it on to our competitors and/or their potential new employer. Once again, you need to have systems in place to prevent this and to make absolutely certain that those who leave have no further access to servers, mailboxes, etc., after they have left. You would be amazed how often ex-employees can still read their emails and other sensitive information months after they have closed the door of your office for the final time.

It also pays to check who the shareholders of your most important suppliers are. Once I discovered that some of my own colleagues were shareholders in one of our key suppliers. Obviously, this is not a healthy situation. It inevitably gives rise to questions – justifiably or not – about how this supplier first came to acquire his preferential position. This kind of speculation is best avoided.

Of course, security matters do not always involve huge sums of money, sensitive data and company secrets. In one of our offices, we were baffled by the 'great toilet paper mystery'. We noted that abnormal amounts of toilet paper were being used (or going missing) month after month. Investigation eventually revealed that one of our members of staff was taking home several rolls every day. Okay, this did not represent a large amount of money, but it did represent a major breach of trust.

Then there are the 'classics'. Staff who abuse the procedures for taking annual leave. Or staff who use the company gas card to fill the tanks of everyone in their family. If someone who works in your office all day is using as much gas as one of your lorry drivers, you know that something is wrong. Moreover, this is a clear example of fraud – no more and no less – and the amount of money involved can soon add up to quite a significant sum. It has always amazed me that some people think that they are going to get away with this kind of thing indefinitely, without anybody noticing.

In the final analysis, it is probably a good idea for every company to set up an effective department for internal control from day one. You will often hear entrepreneurs say: 'But that kind of thing will never happen in my company!' Which is also what I thought when I started out as an entrepreneur. But I was wrong. And so are they. It happens everywhere and the consequences can be far-reaching. Financial damage is one thing, but a loss of confidence in your company can represent a much bigger threat in the long term. So be on your guard against unprincipled behavior of all kinds and set up procedures that strike the right balance between trust and control.

Don't trust everything you see. Even salt looks like sugar.

– *Narges Obaid*

28 The Schumacher of Excel

I am fascinated by figures. I always have been. Which explains why I was as happy as a kid on Christmas Day when I first discovered a tool in the form of a spreadsheet: Excel.

At first, I was nothing special when it came to using it. But after I had followed a supplementary course in Business Administration at the University of Antwerp, Excel became my secret weapon. As part of the course, we needed to analyze business cases, making the necessary calculations quickly and efficiently.

It was a few of my fellow students – civil engineers who were already familiar with the tool – who showed me what Excel can really do. Suddenly a whole new world was opened up for me. I analyzed how the engineers developed their spreadsheets, then went out and bought a number of books on the subject, and instantly became a fanatic. Six months later, I was proficient in its use. Very, very proficient. So much so that my fellow students gave me the nickname of 'the Schumacher of Excel', a reference to the Formula 1 racing driver, who at that time was unbeatable.

This thorough knowledge of Excel has really helped me in my career. I can still recall a training course at one of the banks where I worked. We had to take part in a business game. A fictional bank was put at our disposal and we were supposed to compete with rival banks in a fictional economic environment over a period of a week.

The market situation changed from day to day and we were supposed to take decisions about matters such as price setting, marketing, balance management, etc. This involved a huge amount of calculation work to simulate how the bank could most effectively operate under the new circumstances. The other groups made these calculations manually. This meant that it not only took them ages, but also that they made a number of crucial mistakes. In our group, it was agreed that I should make the calculations using an Excel macro of my own devising, which could simulate all possible scenarios quickly and accurately. This saved our group a huge amount of time – which we spent in the bar. After three days, all the other banks were bankrupt. Ours was the only one that remained. The Schumacher of Excel had done it again!

Years later, a trainee in one of my companies had to make an Excel account. I thought I would show him how. A piece of cake for the Schumacher of Excel! 'Watch and learn,' I told him. After a while, the trainee asked me timidly what I was doing. I thought he meant that he couldn't follow my skillful manipulation of the formulas, so I slowed the pace. But it soon turned out that I wasn't going too fast for him; I was going too slow! The trainee took over my computer and in fifteen minutes finished the work that I had been struggling with for the past hour. He used open-source macros which he adjusted as appropriate.

This incident taught me an important lesson. In my head, I still believed that I was super-efficient with Excel. I was still Schumacher, the undisputed number one. Of course, Schumacher has not been number one for many years now. The new king of Formula 1 is Lewis Hamilton. I was so convinced that what I was doing was right that I failed to keep abreast of the latest tools and the newest technologies. I was efficient in the world of yesterday, when evolution was linear. For me, this was a real wake-up call. In other words, as an entrepreneur, you need to make sure that you don't wait too long before going in search of your own Schumacher killer. In today's world, evolution is exponential.

29 The lift

In Australia, Clear2Pay had fantastic office premises in Sydney. The board room on the top floor had a magnificent view over the world-famous Sydney Opera House. It took a while for the lift to get to this top floor, but at least it gave you the opportunity to chat with some of the local staff on the way up. People I would otherwise not normally have seen.

One day I found myself in the lift with two young men who both wore Clear2Pay badges around their necks. They were discussing a problem with one of their projects. When I asked them precisely what they did in the company, one of them looked at me irritably and said: 'That's none of your damned business!' I wasn't wearing my own badge and was dressed in a Hard Rock t-shirt and sneakers (my normal work uniform when I don't have scheduled meetings with customers). You could see the young man thinking: 'Who the hell is this guy? And why is he trying to poke his nose into matters that don't concern him?'

Later that same day, we had an internal meeting where different teams were required to give a report on the current state of their projects. Just before the meeting started, who should enter the hall? Precisely! Mr. 'That's none of your damned business!' When he saw me and realized that I was the founder of the company, his face turned bright red. And when I gave him a sly wink to show him that I recognized him, he probably saw his career going up in smoke! Fortunately for him, I am not a vindictive person. When I got to know him better, he turned out to be one of our very best project managers. Later, we often laughed about how we first met in the lift.

This may just seem like a harmless anecdote, but it actually got me thinking about a more important matter. It is often the case that people who have been working in a company for a long time do not know who their senior managers are, and vice versa. This is not a healthy situation. If you are working hard to achieve particular objectives, you really need to know who set those objectives in the first place.

On the back of this incident, I decided that from then on, every time I visited one of our foreign offices, I would organize a meeting with the employees recruited during the previous six months irrespective of their role and their position in the company hierarchy. I also made a point of visiting each of these overseas offices at least twice a year.

I let it be known that the new employees could submit questions to me in advance anonymously. I promised to answer those questions openly and transparently during the subsequent meeting. There were no taboo subjects.

I also tasked the HR department with putting together a 'welcome' package for new recruits. The package was designed to contain as much practical information as possible: the history of the company, its structure, its culture, its products, its strategy, etc. Companies often assume that their employees know all these things, but they don't.

Included in each package was also a copy of the latest versions of all the company's policies, as well as photos and short biographies of all the senior managers. The mission statement and vision were positioned prominently on the first page.

This package played a key role in familiarizing our new people with the company's values and philosophy right from the very first day. It not only gave the 'newbies' a strong impression of our professionalism, but also helped them to feel immediately welcome and at home. Of course, a company culture can only be properly assimilated on the workfloor, by actually participating in the company's activities, but you can certainly give this process a helping hand. And that is exactly what our welcome package did.

30 The fifty-million dollar model

At the end of 2008, I wanted to take my company to the next level. To make this possible would require a massive injection of new capital, so that we could go full steam ahead on a far-reaching process of internationalization: takeovers, new product lines, new markets, etc.

The board of directors, which contained several members with international experience, thought I had gone mad when I announced my intention to seek an additional 50 million dollars of capital from an American investor. A representative of one of the investment funds asked me straight to my face whether or not I was suffering from delusions of grandeur. He snarled that I didn't know what I was talking about and that I would not be able to raise a red cent!

But I refused to be intimidated. I had worked in the US and had a good network in New York. I had no intention of being frightened off by an investor who had never set foot outside of Belgium.

Before I got on the plane to America, I thought long and hard about the right strategy. There was no point in just knocking on the door of any old investment house on Wall Street. I had made a list of six funds that had previously shown interest in our kind of company: a software company that sold to financial institutions. At that time, fintech was not the shining star it would later rise to become and there were no specific fintech funds.

American investors are different from their European counterparts. In Europe investors are polite; they explain to you, almost apologetically, why they are not going to invest in your company. In America, the 'time is money' rule applies: if you have not managed to interest them after the first five minutes, you will soon find yourself back out on the street. In other words, you need to grab their attention and grab it fast. So how do you do it?

American investors love figures, statistics and models; preferably models that are visual and easy to understand. In Clear2Pay I had developed a clear model for how the business should be run, which also made clear to our managers just how well or badly they were performing. The model fit on a single slide.

It was with this slide that I was able to convince American investors to inject 50 million dollars into our company.

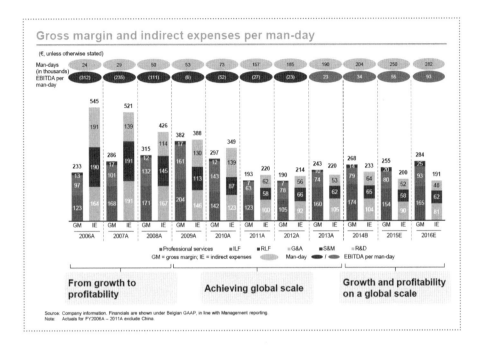

The model looks complex and technical, but that is not the case. Let me explain how it works, as far as this is possible in a book.

With the slide illustrated here (you can find the slide in color at the back of the book) – which contains the same model as the one I showed to the US investors in 2009 – we sold Clear2Pay to FIS in 2014. The model starts in 2006 and continues until 2016. Up to and including 2013, the figures are actual figures. The figures for 2014 are budget figures.

At the top, the number of working days of the staff that directly generate revenue is circled in grey. In other words, not the people in sales, research or administration, but people in departments like, for example, development.

An employee has on average 200 working days per year at his or her disposal. The 24,000 working days noted for 2006 therefore represent roughly 120 employees. You can see that the number of working days increases each year, to more than 290,000 in 2016, equivalent to a workforce of 1,450 revenue-generating employees. In other words, a twelvefold increase in comparison with ten years earlier.

This number of working days is the motor for the entire model. To chart its progress, we developed a system of time registration: employees kept a record of how much time they spent on each project, something similar to what they do in a lawyer's office to calculate billable hours.

For each year in the model there are two separate columns. The left column shows money coming in; the right column shows money going out. Inflow and outflow. The left column consists of three distinct elements: professional services, LIF (license income), and RIF (maintenance income).

The total amount for professional services needs to be reduced by the costs (cost of sales, which is mainly the salary cost) associated with the provision of these services. The result of this calculation is the added value or contribution. This amount is then divided by the motor (the number of revenue-generating days). The slide shows that in 2006 we had a contribution or margin of 123 euros for each working day. Or to express it differently, if an employee cost the company 500 euros per day, his services to others were sold for an amount of 623 euros per day.

The same exercise can be carried out for licenses and maintenance, although in both cases the cost of sales is significantly lower or even non-existent. In 2006, the contribution for licenses amounted to 97 euros per day, whereas the comparable figure for maintenance was 13 euros. In other words, in 2006 each employee generated an added value of 233 euros per day (123 euros + 97 euros + 13 euros).

The right column is also divided into three distinct elements: General & Administration (G&A), Research and Development (R&D), and Sales and Marketing (S&M). The absolute amount for each element is obtained from the analytical accounts, with each figure again being divided by the number of working days. This reveals that in 2006 the company spent average daily amounts of 164 euros on G&A, 191 euros on R&D and 190 euros on S&M, giving a total of 545 euros per working day.

To calculate the overall results, all you need to do is subtract the costs from the income. This shows that in 2006 our balance was in the red. More money was going out of the company than was coming in, to the tune of an average of 312 euros per working day. If you multiply this daily loss by the total number of working days, you end up with the company's total debit for the year. In 2006, this amounted to approximately 7.5 million euros (24,000 working days x a loss of 312 euros per day).

The model makes clear that the situation in 2006 was far from good. The added value from services was too low and both licensing and maintenance yielded insufficient income. At the same time, the company was engaged in developing its sales structure and was investing heavily in R&D.

From this same single slide you can also identify the actions taken by the management in the following years to correct this situation. We opted to alternate periods of growth with periods of improved profitability. This explains why the number of revenue-generating days increases significantly in some years and hardly at all in others, a wave-like pattern that can be seen repeated more than once.

In the years when the number of working days hardly increased, the added value for services rose dramatically. In these years, the focus was on boosting the contribution. How can you do this? Either by increasing your prices or by doing the same amount of work with fewer people. In short, efficiency gains. The real top-class companies combine growth and greater efficiency in the same year, but we were not yet in a position to do this.

By the end of 2009, the moment of truth for Clear2Pay had arrived. We were getting close to the point of breaking even. Our contribution per working day had risen to 204 euros for services and 161 euros for licenses, while the total costs had fallen to 388 euros per working day. As a result, our overall loss was now down to just 6 euros per working day. With a total of some 25,000 working days, this meant a total company loss of scarcely 300,000 euros.

Our single slide makes it possible to see at a glance how our company tripled in size in just three years (from 53,000 working days to 157,000 working days), thanks in part to organic growth but also in part to the 50 million dollars invested by Aquiline, which allowed us to make a number of takeovers.

The model also shows how the following year that growth pushed our margin back into the red. However, we were confident that we were in a position that would allow us to return to a contribution of around 200 euros per day for our services.

By 2013, we were making a profit again: 23 euros per working day. By now, we also had roughly 190,000 working days and were therefore able to realize an EBITDA of some 4.4 million euros.

These figures convinced our prospective buyer that Clear2Pay was a cash machine. If we could increase our margin by 100 euros per working day (which was not an over-ambitious target), we would generate an EBITDA increase of 19 million euros with the same revenue.

This simple calculation was enough to convince the candidate buyer – who was specialized in the optimization of services – to purchase our company for 500 million dollars. But this would not have been possible without our simple model, because without it the buyer would have had to make his decision based on the relatively low EBITDA, which would have made it difficult to assess Clear2Pay's long-term potential. In short, we didn't sell an existing company; we sold a future company. On the basis of a single model. On a single slide.

I have often thought about commercializing this model, but so far have never got around to it. Perhaps it is an idea for my next (ad)venture?

Two things define you.
Your patience when
you have nothing,
and your attitude when
you have everything.

– George Bernard Shaw

31 Mickey Mouse

I sit on various boards of directors. They display huge differences in terms of quality, method, and efficiency. Some entrepreneurs see the board as a talking shop – a consultative body where everybody can have their say – or, even worse, as a necessary evil, which they want to put behind them as quickly as possible. This is a great pity, because a well functioning board of directors is worth its weight in gold.

Getting off to an early start is half the battle. Most companies only set up a formal board of directors when they attract their first serious boost of external capital. But by then it is too late. Every company needs a board of directors from day one, or at the very least some kind of advisory council. There should also be a charter that clearly describes the role, function and structure of this body.

It goes without saying that the shareholders must be represented on the board. But it is also vital to have a number of external members who have no direct connection with the company and can give frank and honest opinions, without there being any question of a conflict of interest.

You need to think carefully about how you select these independent directors. Make a list of potential candidates and contact other companies where they have sat on the board to ask whether or not they participated actively in meetings and yielded an added value. This kind of reference check is by no means a luxury. Lots of directors take the job seriously but I have l known others whose only participation in board meetings consisted of drinking cups of coffee and occasionally asking an intelligent question. Or, more often than not, an unintelligent one.

In one of the companies I founded, I once had the feeling that most of the board members were not taking the trouble to look through the documentation sent to them before the meetings. They all swore blind that they took the necessary time to prepare thoroughly, but that wasn't the impression they gave once they were inside the boardroom.

I couldn't resist the temptation of putting them to the test. For the next meeting, I sent around a folder of documents as usual, but in the middle of it I added a picture of Mickey Mouse. And guess what! Only one of the directors called me up to ask if I had been drinking too much! All the others never said a word, making it clear that they had never even looked at their folder. It gave me the excuse I needed to replace a number of them.

Efficient board meetings

Having a strong board of directors with the right people is step one. Step two is to make sure that you have efficient board meetings. I would pay a lot of money for a tool that could immobilize internet connections for a radius of fifteen meters around a boardroom and that could be activated by the CEO at his or her discretion. Nothing irritates me more than to see board members playing games on their cell phone, or booking their next holiday, or chatting with their latest conquest. This shows little or no respect for the company management.

I make my directors really work. Not only do they often have more time on their hands than my operational managers, it is also logical (at least to me) that they should be involved in the development of certain plans and strategies. Moreover, it is what many directors prefer. They want to work; they want to create added value for the company. So make them happy and let them do it!

Boards of directors usually meet four times a year. In addition to the formal agenda, I zoom in on one extra topic per meeting, worked out in detail by the responsible manager. At the beginning of the year, we discuss the sales strategy for the coming twelve months. In April, the focus shifts to R&D. In July, it is the turn of operations and human resources. In November, the annual audit and the budget for the following year take center stage.

At each meeting, it is the manager of the department in question who comes to give chapter and verse on his or her specialization: the sales manager, the HR manager, the R&D manager, etc. In this way, the managers come into contact with the board members, which makes them feel much more appreciated within the company.

I always try to organize the meetings of the board on our company premises (including our international offices), and not in some boring meeting room in an equally boring hotel alongside a godforsaken motorway in the middle of nowhere. Why? Because in my opinion it is important that the members of the board get to see and experience the company and its culture first hand.

This helps them to better understand the direction in which the company wishes to move, as well as giving them a sense of its strengths and weaknesses. In short, it helps to bring the tedious tables of facts and figures in their board pack to life.

The board pack

If you want to have efficient board meetings, it is important to have a high-quality board pack: the documentation that forms the central thread running through the meeting. When I am considering an investment in a new company, I always ask to see examples of their board packs. These can tell you a lot about the way a company is run.

What are the elements that help to make a good board pack? Here are some useful rules of thumb:

- Send the documentation to board members at least five days before the meeting is scheduled. Many entrepreneurs have a thousand-and-one other things to do and preparing the documentation for the board meeting is often the least of their worries. As a result, they hurriedly throw a board pack together without much thought and send it off at the very last minute. As a director myself, I am a stickler for getting the necessary documentation in good time, so that I can study it thoroughly. I want to be able to fulfill my task properly.

- Ensure that the documentation is coherent. Board packs are often a hastily prepared collection of unrelated documents, in which it is hard to see a consistent line. They are often written in different styles and printed in different layouts with different fonts. Some are short and to the point; others are long and detailed. This creates a highly unprofessional impression. Remember that the board pack will be going into your company archives and may be necessary later for due diligence or some other reason. So make sure that it does your company credit, rather than discredit.

- The board pack starts with an agenda. Try to give a time indication alongside each point, so that the chairman of the board can keep an eye on how the timing of the meeting is progressing. Always put the most important points at the top of the agenda. I have been in board meetings where the management set the most contentious issues at the bottom of the agenda, in the hope that the meeting would run out of time to discuss them properly. This often related to matters such as stock options, bonuses, or salary increases. When I saw this tactic being applied, I was never afraid to ask the chairman to turn the agenda on its head, so that we could start with these issues – much to the annoyance of the managers whose trick I had seen through.

- Immediately after the agenda, it is best to give a summary of the different KPIs (Key Performance Indicators) that are important for the company: revenue, available cash reserves, new customers, retention, churn, number of staff, etc.
  These KPIs sketch the necessary background for the 'state of the union', in which the CEO outlines the most important activities, achievements, and challenges of the previous quarter. This state of the union must give all the directors a clear impression of how the company has performed during the previous three months.

- After these introductory elements, it is next customary to review the action list relating to the matters agreed at the previous board meeting. Every action to be taken is given a sequential number and allocated to a responsible manager. The new meeting runs through the matters that have not yet been actioned.

- The core of the board pack is made up from the classic elements of all board meetings: the financial figures, a status check on R&D, a summary of projects in progress, the results of marketing actions, an analysis of the sales process, and a summary of the personnel who have joined and left the company since the last meeting.

- It may seem like a detail, but don't forget to add a copy of the minutes of the previous meeting. These need to be approved and signed at the start of the new meeting. Many companies overlook this need for signing, and as a result they have to be 'creative' if their minutes are needed for official purposes at some point in the future.

- I always think it is useful to add a report on the activities of your competitors to the board pack. Are they ahead of you in the market? Are they behind you? What is your company's approach towards them? In this way, the directors get a better impression of the nature and the level of the competition in your sector. This is a useful exercise that obliges you to take a bird's-eye view of the sector and your company's position in it at least once every three months.

- A good board deck consists of no more than twenty slides. It is not the intention to run through this deck slide by slide during the meeting. If you have done your preparation correctly, the members of the board should already be familiar with the basic information they contain, which creates time and space in the meeting to zoom in on strategic questions and issues.

- If there are difficult points on the agenda, it is advisable as the CEO to consult with the board members in advance. It is important to explain to each board member individually why you think particular decisions need to be taken in the interests of the company. A meeting of the board of directors is not the best place to start seeking consensus. You need to do that before the meeting starts.

32 Long live the CFO!

I was not the CEO at Clear2Pay. In fact, I have not been the CEO at any of the companies I have founded. There are two reasons for this. The first is very simple: there are other people who can do it better than I can. The second is something I have already mentioned: I like to work in parallel, which allows me to be active in different companies at the same time. I need variety.

These different challenges and experiences have made me a better entrepreneur. Variety is good for me and good for the companies in which I am involved. But this wearing of many different hats is difficult for a CEO. Investors expect a CEO to be two hundred percent committed to the company he runs. I could only do this if I gave up all my other activities – and I wasn't prepared to take that step.

Because I am good with figures, my first investor in Clear2Pay thought that I should take on the role of CFO. In fact, it was the only remaining position available (all the others had already been filled). I was quite happy with this decision. CFO is an interesting job in a young company. Of course, you need to know something about accounting and the difference between assets and liabilities. But above all you need to know from day one how you can set up and run a well functioning financial structure. If you can do this, you are already half way to success.

It never ceases to amaze me just how few companies have sound financial organization. They have an accountant, but they often have no decent financial department of their own. Their chart of accounts is often illogical and confusing, and very few of them, certainly during the early days, work with an analytical system. It is this latter element that is most crucial of all. Without analytical accounts, your company is effectively flying blind.

With analytical accounts, all the costs incurred by the company are allocated to a particular category of expenditure: Cost of Sales (costs made to generate revenue), General & Administrative costs (G&A), Research & Development (R&D), Sales & Marketing (S&M), etc. By also allocating a portion of your salary costs to each of these posts, you will gain greater insight into your company and see where the money you earn actually goes. And if you ever reach the point of wanting to sell your company, your analytical accounts are the first thing that a prospective buyer will want to see.

I was the CFO of Clear2Pay for more than fifteen years, and I am proud that the Americans who eventually bought the company never withheld a single cent of the guarantee. This was the reward for a number of sound financial practices that I had applied right from the very beginning, so that I can honestly say that I was a good and careful custodian of the company's money.

For example, every quarter I made a summary of all the company's costs, supplier by supplier and listed in order from large to small, right down to the few euros it cost for sandwiches during our business meetings. This kind of summary allows you to identify trends more easily and also makes clear the surprising volume of costs that companies are sometimes required to carry.

Another of my quarterly habits was to have a modest lunch with our banker(s). I told them what was going well with the company and what was going less well. At each meal we examined the latest figures and projections in a fully transparent manner.

In this way, I was able to build up a relationship of trust with our banker(s) who were fully in the picture about developments within the company. They also learned to understand and appreciate just how accurately we were able to assess and make predictions about our business. This was a crucial factor in allowing us to win their confidence. And whether you are a one-man operation, an SME (small and medium-sized enterprise), or a large corporation, it always pays to be on good terms with your banker. Because sooner or later, once you start to grow, you are going to need him or her. If, at that moment, you have a relationship of mutual trust and respect, you will be able to more readily win support for your growth plans.

A third useful habit of mine was to take a folder home at the end of each month, with copies of all the incoming and outgoing invoices. With a glass of good wine at my side, I went through them one by one. Why did we incur that cost? Who decided to authorize that expenditure? Was the final invoice in keeping with the terms of the contract?

This not only helped me to keep in touch with the costs we were incurring but also helped me to track down countless discrepancies that were not in line with our policies as a company. Especially during the early years, when we did not yet have fulltime account controllers, this monthly exercise was very useful. In my experience, people do the strangest things with other people's money. Buying bottles of wine at three hundred euros a shot. Putting in the same claim for expenses twice. Or even forgetting to invoice a customer for our services!

Nobody likes to receive an email from their boss asking them to justify a particular item of expenditure. So I made sure that everyone in the company was well aware of my monthly checking ritual. By keeping a very close watch on things, I applied the necessary pressure to ensure that our people would deal with the company's money sensibly. As a result, we developed a culture where everyone carefully assessed the need for every cost, no matter how small. As the old saying goes, if you take care of the pennies, the pounds will look after themselves.

There are very few companies where the people at the top systematically go through all the invoices. In my opinion, this is a serious and dangerous mistake. Serious because it leads to the development of a culture of financial indifference or even extravagance. Dangerous because you fail to become aware of these excesses until the damage has already been done.

As the CFO, you need to keep your company's finances on a tight rein. Wasteful expenditure and lost income, both great and small, have the potential to bring your company crashing down. Consequently, you need to remain vigilant at all times so that you can correct people's bad habits before it is too late.

33 Listen to your market, your customers, and your mother-in-law

One of the most important qualities of a good entrepreneur and a good company is the ability to adapt. In our rapidly changing digital world, this is truer than ever before. The capacity to quickly and easily modify your behavior in response to new feedback from the market, your competitors, or your customers is fundamental to being successful. And staying successful.

This may sound self-evident, but it isn't. I have seen many companies fail because they stuck stubbornly to their original business idea. Or else they hung on for too long in the sector where they acquired their first important customer. It is seldom the case that your first brilliant product is the product that will later allow you to conquer the market. And that first important customer is not always representative of the customers you need to buy your product in huge numbers. The customers who are crying out for your product might actually be in a completely different market altogether. So don't become too attached to your first product, first sector, or first sale. Instead, be on the lookout constantly for new markets and new opportunities.

The ability to adapt is also crucial when you go in search of funding. Start-ups often invest a huge amount of time in a killer presentation. They hope to knock the socks off potential investors, persuading them to open their wallets and empty out the contents. But investors don't put millions of dollars into companies that stand still.

A presentation intended to raise new capital needs to be a living thing. Feedback (for example, about points that are not clear) and questions from potential investors need to constantly push its development in a different direction. If, after a gap of two months, I see the same presentation from a company that is trying to get me to invest, I know that the mindset of that company is in a bad place. If you haven't learned anything new in two months, that does not bode well for the future.

When I go in search of new funds, I always start (as I have already mentioned) with investors whose money I don't want. All I am interested in is their reaction to my presentation. Their questions tell me a lot about where I need to make changes. This means that when I go to the investors whose money I do want, I am much better prepared and know what to expect. By now, my amended presentation will actually be able to anticipate most of their questions, reflecting what I know they want to hear.

You can't do this straight away. It is only possible if you first actively go in search of feedback and are willing to listen to what it says. Unless you are prepared to expose yourself and your idea to often harsh (but hopefully constructive) criticism and unless you are prepared to take this criticism on board, you will never secure the money you need to make your company grow.

Here is another good tip: don't show your slides immediately to your potential investors; show them first to your mother-in-law instead. A pitch and a presentation must be clear and to the point. Investors and customers don't have a lot of time. They need to understand immediately what problem your product or service is designed to solve. If you don't convince them in the first two minutes, you have lost them for good. But if even your mother-in-law can understand what you are trying to say, you are probably on the right track.

Every company needs to constantly monitor its continuing ability to adapt. As an entrepreneur, you must always be on the look-out for feedback from your customers and the market. You must always keep a close eye on what your competitors are doing and you must always be searching for new opportunities, which you must have the courage to seize. And if you don't do it? Just ask Kodak or Nokia, perhaps the two most famous examples of once powerful world leaders who went under because they rested for too long on their laurels and were unwilling to adjust to the changing world around them.

In companies, vital information often fails to find its way to the right place, certainly when your company starts to grow. Everyone is busy with their own specific tasks and there is seldom enough time for consultation. Consequently, customer feedback tends to get lost or stuck half way. For example, your sales people and customer service teams might know what customers are saying, but this information doesn't always reach the people developing and making the products. As a result, the last opportunity is missed to add desirable new features or remove/amend unsatisfactory old ones before the following product release.

For this reason, every company should appoint a Chief of Feedback, who must collect feedback from customers and staff, ensure its dissemination throughout all levels of the company, and insist on its inclusion as a permanent item on the agenda of the weekly management meeting. In fact, it should probably be the subject with which each meeting begins. Last but not least, the Chief of Feedback must also guarantee that the company does something meaningful with all this valuable feedback. In this sense, the Chief of Feedback is also the Chief of Adaptation.

If plan A doesn't work, the alphabet has 25 more letters.

– Claire Cook

34 Clean-Up-Your-Shit-days

How has your staff evolved since you started your company? How many customers leave each year? Were there fewer last year than the year before? How many customers have you attracted during the past five years in each country where you operate? Every company receives hundreds of questions of this kind. From potential investors, from the authorities who are checking your tax return, from bureaus that are conducting a survey, etc.

It is always fascinating to see how a company deals with these questions. They are often passed around the entire organization, from department to department, like a hot potato that nobody wants to hold. No one knows the answer; no one has the necessary data in usable form. The people who should know have since left the company. The archive in which the information might have been kept recently crashed. Perhaps there are still paper documents in the cellar, but nobody has been down there for the past three years. And if the company has changed premises more than once since its foundation, there is a good chance that this archive – a euphemism for a few tatty shelves and filing cabinets from Ikea – has been lost.

As a result, companies waste a huge amount of time searching for the right information. Sometimes, in desperation and at great cost, they even hire consultants to plough through all their old files and mailboxes.

Companies far too frequently fail to realize that data and information are crucially important assets. Not only to avoid unnecessary fines from the tax man, but also as a guide for making smarter future decisions on the basis of objective facts and figures from the past.

The speed with which a company can retrieve the right data says much about that company's methods of working, structure and organization. If I am considering an investment in a company, I bombard its management with questions. I am not really all that bothered about the actual answers. What interests me is how quickly and how easily they can find the relevant information.

This is an excellent way to check if the engine under the hood is in good working order. If the company can provide the necessary information in a structured way and (even better) in a relatively short space of time, then this, in my book at least, gives a serious boost to its credibility.

As an entrepreneur, how can you best deal with the huge growth and fragmentation of data and information? I have developed a tried and trusted method for all my companies. Each new year is always slow to get started. Nothing much happens in January, except one New Year's reception after another. It is a quiet period. Much too quiet. And very inefficient. Which makes it the ideal moment to organize your Clean-Up-Your-Shit days.

For a few days in January, everyone in the company focuses on collecting and collating all the data from the previous year and converting it into easy to view graphics. Everything comes under the microscope: new employees and new exits, amounts of commission and bonuses paid, new customers and customers who left, customer loyalty, average sales prices, published press articles, audit reports, etc. All this data is then stored in a single (and large) electronic file in the cloud, together with the graphics and the basic raw data.

What's more, by making these graphics the same way year after year, with the same sources and the same methodology, it becomes a simple matter to track down and monitor annual evolutions. This is certainly useful for potential investors, but also for yourself, so that you can perhaps rescue a failing trend or give an additional push to a rising one.

The Clean-Up-Your-Shit operation only lasts for a few days. But you will reap its rewards throughout the entire year.

35 Sticking to the job

In one of the companies where I am a director, the management recently organized a so-called 'all-hands' meeting. Some two hundred employees were gathered together to listen to the company's various senior managers describe their activities during the previous year and outline their plans for the coming one. The aim was to make sure that everyone was working in the same direction and that the different countries and markets were well attuned to each other.

At one point, it was the turn of the sales manager from Germany to give his presentation. He began by asking his audience a question: 'How many of you are involved in sales?' A dozen or so people stood up; the rest remained seated. The manager shook his head and said: 'No, you should all stand up – because everyone in the entire organization is connected in some way, whether directly or indirectly, with sales.' With a simple question and without the use of a single slide, this manager had made a crucial point: sales are the life blood that flows through the veins of every commercial company. And, as is the case with human blood vessels, you are going to find yourself in a lot of trouble if that flow starts to splutter. Your company's chain is only as strong as its weakest link.

Whether we are talking about the receptionist at the front desk who gives all your visitors a warm welcome or the polite man from the accounts department who lets an approaching customer take the last free space in the car park, every member of staff is involved in selling your company. Take, for example, my fantastic personal assistant, Julie Bertjens. She is usually the first person with whom customers or potential customers come into contact. As a result, the way she deals with a customer plays a decisive role in shaping that customer's image of our company. Whether someone remains a customer or not will be determined to a significant degree by that very first contact with Julie. In other words, she is also closely involved in sales.

The sales manager from Germany had a second question – or rather instruction – for his audience. He asked them to look under their seats to see if something was stuck there. During the break he had taped a ten-euro banknote to the bottom of a dozen or so chairs. The people who found the notes waved them in the air, with a big smile on their face. It became an even bigger smile when our friend from Germany told the lucky ones that they could keep the money.

But the sales manager had made yet another very important point. As a company, you are sometimes sitting on top of a pile of money, but you have to get off your backside if you want to find it. In every company new opportunities are coming and going all the time. Sometimes you only need to take a single step to pluck them out of the air before they disappear. But this means, of course, that you need to keep your eyes open and must always be on the alert. I regularly meet people who tell me that they would like to be an entrepreneur, but are convinced that everything worthwhile has already been discovered or invented. In other words, that there are no new opportunities. What nonsense!

Between the lines, our German friend also made a third important point: you don't need a hundred slides to make an impact on an audience. His presentation was the shortest of the day, but it was the one that everyone went home remembering.

36 Getting the most out of your sales pipeline

One of the companies I am involved with makes a short video every time a big deal is landed. In the video, someone bangs a gong and then gives a brief explanation about the deal: the customer, the product, the cost, etc. The video is then loaded onto WhatsApp and circulated throughout the company. As a result, everyone is aware of the company's latest commercial success which works wonders for staff morale.

Unfortunately, too many companies pay too little attention to the sales side of their operations. As a result, it is sometimes difficult for investors to get a clear picture of what deals are in the sales pipeline, even though this is one of the most important parameters for assessing how well or how poorly a company is performing.

Some companies are aware of this and attempt to throw sand in the eyes of their investors by repeatedly changing the way they record and report their sales pipeline data. As an investor, you can avoid this pitfall by securing agreement in your investment contract that the relevant metrics can only be changed with the approval of the board of directors. Other companies are more honest, but even then they can't always tell you what is in their sales pipeline because sometimes they don't really know.

I am not in favor of a weighted sales pipeline. You can compare this with the supply of water to your home. There is always water in the pipes, but it is only of use to you when you turn the tap and it flows into your bath. It is the same with business deals: you can have hundreds in the pipeline, but what are they worth to your company if most of them only have little chance of success?

I prefer my sales managers to report how much a deal is worth and when it is likely to be concluded. Size and timing are the crucial parameters in every sales pipeline.

In order to have a clear picture and make a predictive model, every new deal added to the sales pipeline must be given a unique code, consisting of the year, month and sequential number within that month.

In this way, you can know how many deals are still in the pipeline and also assess the feasibility of their targets. If by the end of the second quarter you have only booked 5 million in sales when your target for the year was 12 million, you can immediately think about ways to try and make good the potential shortfall. Are there still enough winnable deals in the pipeline to earn 7 million in the next six months? Or do you need to make an extra effort to find new prospects? Or can you perhaps upsell to existing customers? Without a clear picture of your pipeline, you are flying blind.

I have developed the habit of making a monthly summary of all the deals won and lost, which I order from large to small. In this way, you keep in touch with what is happening in your customer portfolio. You know who your most important customers are and also where you need to make an extra investment.

If a customer asks you to provide extra features for your product, you can instantly see whether or not it is worth making the effort. Does he buy enough to make the extra development profitable? With lost deals, it is also important to try and find out why you lost. If the customer simply decides to postpone the purchase, there is not a lot that you can do about it. But if he says that your price is too high? Or too low (which can sometimes be the case)? Or that a rival product was better? You can learn lessons from every lost deal.

Thanks to the use of sequential numbers, you know exactly when a deal entered the sales pipeline, also which deals need to be removed because they have been there for too long without showing any signs of life. There is no point in carrying too much dead wood. So make sure that you clean out your sales pipeline at least twice every year.

I have never worked
a day in my life without
selling. If I believe
in something, I sell it,
and I sell it hard.

– *Estée Lauder*

37   Tame the meeting tigers

One of the most curious phenomena about a company that grows is that the number of the meetings also grows. What's more, the short, informal meetings of the start-up period are replaced by long, formal meetings that seem to involve a continuously increasing number of participants, usually reaching the conclusion after the meeting that nothing meaningful was decided. Or even worse still, that nobody really knew the purpose of the meeting in the first place. In this way, growing companies unconsciously develop a meeting culture, which eats away at the company's efficiency and productivity.

There came point in time when I suddenly realized that most weeks my diary was packed solid with planned meetings from Monday morning to Friday afternoon. Many of them were internal meetings. All I did was rush from one meeting venue to another. My level of efficiency plummeted while my levels of frustration and stress sky-rocketed.

I also came to see that some people had transformed the nature of their job, so that they were now 'meeting professionals'. It made no difference whether the meeting was useful or not, or whether their presence was necessary or not: they were always there. I called them the meeting tigers.

It irritated me that more and more of the meetings I was forced to attend ended up in hours of fruitless discussion. The meeting tigers had refined 'discussion for discussion's sake' into a fine art. It was their way of justifying their position at the table. They were saying: 'Hey, look at me. I'm here as well!'

It couldn't be allowed to carry on like this. The more meetings we held, the worse our results seemed to get. Something had to be done.

My solution was as a radical as it was pragmatic. I issued every member of staff with a personal identification code. For every internal meeting involving more than four people, I instructed that each attendee had to enter his or her code into a computer before the meeting started.

Our self-written computer program automatically projected the calculated salary cost of those present onto a large screen. This cost was adjusted on a minute-by-minute basis in real time. As a result, everyone in the room could see what the meeting was costing the company. The longer the meeting, the greater the cost.

I left it up to the meeting's participants to decide whether or not their meeting was worth its cost. In most instances, that turned out not to be the case. In fact, many managers were genuinely shocked when they saw in black and white just how much of the company's money was being gobbled up by these meetings.

Result? The number of meetings soon began to fall drastically and the remaining meetings were conducted much more efficiently, with fewer participants, more decisions and more concrete action points. The days of endless discussion were a thing of the past. The meeting tigers had been tamed.

38 Buy a scanner

One of the best investments that any starting company can make costs just a few hundred dollars: a decent scanner; a machine that can digitalize all your documents quickly and easily. You don't have a few hundred dollars? In the worst case scenario you can use your smartphone to make your scans. There are good apps for as little as a few dollars that make this possible.

The first years of a new company are often characterized by chaos and a lack of structure. You have too little time and too much to do. Making neat collections of all your documents is not your greatest priority. As a result, an increasingly large pile of documents, some of them important, grows and grows on your desk. But when the time comes for your thriving company to move to bigger and better premises, this pile (and everyone else's pile) gets packed away into boxes, most of which disappear into the corner of a cellar, never to see the light of day again.

Your company continues to thrive, so much so that you now need new capital for further expansion. Your potential investor is interested, but asks to see all your original documents. Disaster! The notes that you scribbled on the boxes all those years ago before throwing them into cellar are no longer legible. Or if they are, they are no longer accurate. Where on earth are your foundation documents, key contracts, share option agreements and all the rest? Have you, in fact, still got them or were they lost during the move or mistakenly thrown out during a subsequent 'Clean-Up-Your-Shit' operation?

Panic and stress! Suddenly, it is all hands on deck to try and find the missing documents. An inventory would help, of course, but you never got around to making one. So now you have to plough through every box manually, which may take so much time that your funding round needs to be delayed. Perhaps for months. Perhaps permanently. If only you had bought that scanner ...

Admittedly, it is not the most challenging job and there will always be more pressing claims on your time. Even so, you really should make an effort to keep your documents in a structured manner from day one. Not in boxes that can get lost, or ruined when your cellar floods, or eaten by mice. No, you must do it digitally and send it to the cloud with a reliable backup.

Work methodically. Use a structure that allows a separate section with a separate electronic file for each part of the company (HR, finance, legal, IT, etc.). In this way, every document can be placed in the right file with an identifying code (year/month/number). You can find an example of a possible structure in annex 1 at the back of the book. In the jargon this is known as a data room and it can offer a useful structure both for storage in the cloud and for physical storage. The way you arrange things will ultimately depend on your personal preferences, but make sure that whatever system you use allows you to find documents quickly and easily.

If you follow this simple and relatively inexpensive rule, you won't need to turn your entire company upside down whenever an investor asks to see this or that document. It will save the investor irritation and your own staff hours of valuable time. Moreover, by giving your investor access to your database in the cloud during due diligence, you can monitor which documents he is consulting. Is he serious about giving you money or is he just stringing you along? The documents he examines should give you the answer.

39 Unknown is unloved

When I first started my career as an entrepreneur, people in my environment nodded sympathetically. They thought that my effort to create a new company from scratch was 'bold'. In most cases, however, 'bold' was just a polite way of saying that, in their opinion, I didn't stand a chance.

This changed the moment I got an interview in the newspapers, complete with a large photo. I could see friends and acquaintances looking at me in a new way. It was as if I had risen in their estimation. They now started to take my company seriously. This reaction was totally irrational but nonetheless real. It proved the magic – or rather the power – of the press.

Perception is reality. My company was doing just as well before the newspaper article as it did afterwards. But in the eyes of many people I had been transformed from a naïve adventurer into a successful businessman. In fact, I was neither, but it demonstrated the power of the media to influence people's thinking. It was a lesson that I was quick to learn.

Many entrepreneurs prefer to keep a low profile, particularly in Flanders. Even so, media attention can help to move your company forward in leaps and bounds. Not by giving your ego a boost, but by increasing your credibility in the eyes of your employees, your customers and your investors.

Of course, attracting this attention is not easy, especially for a young start-up that nobody has ever heard of. How do you get your name into the paper, on the radio, or on television? I started by conducting a small-scale market research study and linking this to my own company and product. Journalists love market research and the figures it produces. Just open any newspaper and you will see headlines like 'Nine out of every ten Belgians say ...' or 'X percent of consumers use ...'.

Once you have done your market research, send it off to every journalist you know, accompanied by an explanatory text that even the busiest reporter can easily incorporate into a ready-made article.

This is step one. But remember that building a reputation takes time. You are not going to get front-page coverage in *Forbes* or *The Economist* straight away. Be content to start off modestly. The first article about my company appeared in our local newspaper. Next time, we managed to get a mention in the national press. That is the best way to get your name noticed: one step at a time.

After this has happened a few times, you may find the roles being reversed: instead of you looking for the press, the press come looking for you. They want to know something about your market or the technology you use. This generates a kind of snowball effect, so that after a while, journalists come to regard you as the 'expert' in your sector. Which, of course, helps even more to turn the media spotlight on your own company.

I began to invest early on in developing good relations with journalists. I regarded them as important customers. Admittedly, they can sometimes do annoying things and on occasions they make impossible demands. But you have to remain friendly and keep on the right side of them. Remember that they can do you harm as well as good.

You need to build up a relationship of mutual trust with journalists. They must be able to rely on you to give them information that is accurate and credible. In return, you must be able to rely on them to report your words correctly and without revealing confidential information that you may have given them off the record.

It serves both your interests not to breach this trust. If you find that a journalist is not playing by the rules, next time give your story to a journalist in a rival medium. On the reverse side of the coin, it goes without saying that all the information you give to a journalist must be true. If she or he discovers that you are feeding them 'fake news', they will never mention your company again, unless in a negative way.

I sometimes give interviews in a restaurant or bar. This allows you to get to know the journalist in a different and more informal setting. You must prepare these interviews (and any other conversations with the press) thoroughly. I always try to imagine what they are likely to ask – especially the difficult questions that I would prefer them not to ask – and then work out the best possible answers.

When you are dealing with journalists, impulsiveness and improvization should be avoided at all costs.

There are two standard tactics to attract the attention of the media. You can send out a press release, for which you require a list of relevant journalists that you dig out of your bottom drawer whenever you have something new and interesting to tell. Alternatively, you can give your news exclusively to just a single medium or reporter. Journalists are always trying to beat their rivals to a good story. If you offer them an exclusive, you are bound to get prominent coverage, much more so than if you were to share the same information with all your press contacts. Important tip: always ask if you can read the article before publication, so that you can ask that flagrant errors (wrong figures, misquotations, etc.) are corrected.

The journalists I know are all competent, reliable, and trustworthy people. Even so, you always need to be on your guard. The press can make or break your company's reputation. There are enough examples of entrepreneurs who have first been praised to the heavens by the media, only to be later condemned to the outer circles of hell by the same media, sometimes even by the same journalists. For this reason, I seldom give figures and prognoses to reporters and I never make statements that I am not able to verify, or claims that I am not able to make good. Pride cometh before a fall ...

Always try to be authentic when dealing with the press. Failure is an inevitable part of any entrepreneur's career, so from time to time your company will get things wrong. Don't be afraid to make this public. If you are open and transparent, you will be able to keep one step ahead of the journalists and steal some of their thunder.

I have never worked with a PR agency. For me, it is important to maintain a personal relationship with journalists. They look at your company and your sector from a different perspective and this often yields interesting insights that can be useful to you and your company. Besides, you don't really need to pay PR people to get your name in the newspapers. If your story is interesting enough – and it is up to you to make it interesting – the journalists will know how to find you.

Remember also that building credibility requires more than just media attention. For this reason, over the years I have spent much time and energy giving lectures and keynotes to students, business leaders, societies and associations, often as frequently as once per week. This offers numerous benefits. First and foremost, it allows you to build and extend an interesting network. But talking with others, particularly business leaders, has also helped me to bring my own story into sharper focus.

You need to keep an audience engaged, which means that you need to tell them a story that is both interesting and inspiring. Storytelling is hugely important. It helps to set in motion a snowball of reactions that keeps getting bigger and bigger all the time. A good story ultimately provides more customers, more media attention and more investors.

Yes, even investors can be swayed by the magic of the press. Just as family and friends started to look at me differently after that first article in the local paper, so too with investors: they attach much more weight to your name once it has been mentioned in the media. You are shown more respect and gain greater credibility. Suddenly, your story is believed. In our case, this was wholly irrational, because the article in question only dealt with a small part of our company's activities. Which all goes to prove that even investors sometimes take decisions based on irrational behavior.

40   Twenty percent effort, eighty percent result

Have you ever heard of Self-Enhancement Bias? This is the belief that you do everything better than everyone else, so that it is ultimately easier to do everything yourself. Self-Enhancement Bias is fatal for an entrepreneur. To build a successful company, it is essential that you delegate.

I am a strong believer in the Pareto principle, which says that you achieve eighty percent of your result with twenty percent of your effort. The secret is knowing yourself sufficiently well to be able to identify the twenty percent of your work at which you are unquestionably the best. Management? Strategy? Budgeting? Recruitment? Focus on your strengths and delegate the remaining eighty percent to your team.

As a starter-entrepreneur, this was something I found hard to do. I had to learn how to delegate and even today I have the tendency to want to do things myself. When you start up a company, you are responsible for just about everything, from strategy to sending out the invoices, and from sales to filling up the coffee machine. In these early days, it is not only the broad lines of policy but also the daily details of operational matters that end up on your plate. You constantly need to juggle these different roles.

Once the company begins to grow and you take on more staff, you have the option to delegate more. Like me, not every entrepreneur finds this easy. You lose part of your control and your oversight. You must learn to be patient. Some tasks will take longer, because others first need to become familiar with them.

You will also discover that some of the work will be done differently (and, in your eyes, worse), but you have to accept this and let it pass. Delegation is about giving trust. If you are always looking over your employees' shoulders and rapping them on the knuckles, you might as well just carry on doing everything yourself. In this way, of course, you will never gain any additional time for yourself. Because that is the purpose of delegation: to create time for yourself as an entrepreneur to do the things at which you can excel and where you can generate most added value for your company.

Delegation not only benefits you personally, it also benefits the people to whom you delegate. Showing that you have confidence in them, will increase their motivation and improves the general working atmosphere. This is particularly the case when the employees know that the tasks in question are tasks that you like doing and think are important.

An important instrument for streamlining the delegation of tasks is the so-called DOA or Delegation Of Authority. In a DOA you divide up the work and determine how much responsibility and autonomy you wish to give to your employees for the performance of the delegated tasks. Consequently, you don't just set them tasks; you give them authority to do those tasks as they see fit.

Many companies do not have clear DOAs. They might sometimes have one for bank transactions, in which, for example, they specify the limits for which certain officials can authorize expenditure without the need for a second counter-signature. But often that is all, even though DOAs are just as important for matters relating to investments, operational costs, sales, loans, personnel, etc.

DOAs are 'living' documents – or should be. Sometimes companies have DOAs but never amend them to reflect changing circumstances, such as scale and market conditions. This is necessary, because a DOA in a small starter company often looks very different from a DOA in a fast-growing international company.

Another frequent mistake is that the DOA is linked to the name of a member of staff rather than to a function. If the member of staff leaves the company, the DOA is immediately rendered useless.

Delegation is necessary if you want your company to grow. And as the old saying goes, good agreements make good friends. A DOA that clearly defines an employee's room to maneuver can help to avoid frustrations – not only for the employee, but also for you!

An example of a DOA can be found in annex 2.

41 Fire fast and hire slow

I would much prefer to have a bad product and a good team than a good product and a bad team. A strong team will always find a way to make that bad product better, while a bad team is guaranteed to ruin the prospects of even the best product.

Good employees are the core of every company, but they are incredibly hard to find. For me, learning how to attract the right talent was a long and painful process.

Initially, you look at the CV that is sent you. This usually describes in full and in detail what the candidate has done so far in his or her life and career. You often get the impression that you are dealing with a superman or woman. Sadly, I have learned (at my expense) that many people are economical with the truth when it comes to writing their CV. For this reason, I now apply (and have done so for many years) a number of recruitment rules from which I never deviate.

Rule one: ask for a copy of their qualifications (school, college, university, etc.). With roughly one out of every ten candidates you will discover that there is something wrong with their diploma. They often don't have one or, if they do, it is not the one they list on their CV. They may well have started the course in question, but never completed it. The fact that they lie about their qualifications immediately makes me suspicious. If they can't be honest about their education and training, what else might they be hiding?

People like to portray themselves as being different (and usually better) than they are. That is human nature. But do you really want to risk your credibility with a potential new employer by telling a few stupid white lies? Just tell the truth!

Rule two: ask for and check references. I always check at least three, including people not suggested by the candidate. These reference checks often reveal new and unexpected insights. For example, that the candidate was only marginally involved in securing the big deal that he boasts about on his CV.

References are the most objective and most reliable source of information. Consciously or unconsciously, we all have the tendency to overestimate ourselves. For this reason, other people are better able to see our weaknesses than we can.

Rule three: ask to see the candidate's last pay slip. This can sometimes be a sensitive issue, but it is necessary to do it. I have interviewed countless candidates who dared to exaggerate the salary package they received at their previous employer. Not just their basic pay, but also the type of company car they had, the pension scheme, expenses, etc.

In addition to the above rules, I also ask all the candidates I see to solve a case. The way they tackle this case is often more important than the actual outcome. A candidate can always claim that he is a brilliant developer, but I prefer to see it with my own eyes.

In one of the software companies where I am a director, candidate-developers need to solve an actual test case. The degree of difficulty is quite high, so that the test is an excellent yardstick. The candidates with the best score frequently go on to become our best developers. If, for whatever reason, we take on someone whose test score was not so good, they usually don't stay with us for very long. Designing a test for your candidates is therefore a very efficient way of recruiting.

For me, a job interview is not just a formality that I want to get finished as quickly as possible. I always ask about the details in the candidate's cv. What did they do in their previous job? What did a typical working day look like? What did they learn? I also always ask what makes them happy. What is their ultimate goal in life? I take a similar interest in their studies and hobbies. What are the sources of their inspiration and passion?

You should take your time when you are recruiting people. That being said, I see lots of companies that do the exact opposite. They recruit quickly and, if things don't work out, they keep the staff concerned on their books for far too long. No company needs this kind of dead wood.

Perhaps it is a cultural thing, but Belgian entrepreneurs are very poor at giving people the sack. They first try to save anything that can be saved from the situation, perhaps with an extra training course for the failing employee. If that doesn't work, maybe an internal transfer will help. Perhaps he will be better in HR? Or what about sales?

If someone does not fit in with your company culture or is simply not good enough, extra training and job rotation won't help. The only solution is to take the bull by the horns and dismiss the person. Do it honestly and correctly, but also quickly.

Especially in a small company, everyone needs to pull their weight and create added value. If a company has five hundred employees, it is not a real problem if employee five hundred and one is a dud. The other five hundred can compensate for his or her deficiencies. But in a company with just ten employees, number eleven also needs to be a bull's-eye.

My motto is therefore 'fire fast and hire slow', whereas most companies do the opposite. In the long run, this makes them weaker. Don't make compromises when it comes to recruitment. Only take on the best possible people and work with them to build the best possible company. If some of your employees are not up to the mark, show them the door. Accept no excuses or extenuating circumstances. They just have to go.

42 Firing people: pity yes, self-pity no

Nothing is more difficult for an entrepreneur than firing people. Often these are colleagues that you have worked with for years and with whom you have built up a relationship of trust. What's more, you know their dismissal will probably have a huge psychological and financial impact on their life.

For this reason, you must never fire someone without first giving it some serious thought. If you feel you have no alternative to a dismissal, prepare it well, plan it thoroughly, and carry it out in a humane and dignified manner.

I am not an HR specialist. Even so, there have been occasions throughout my career when I have had to fire people. This has taught me a number of important lessons, which I am happy to share.

- If it is necessary to fire a number of people – say, for economic reasons – make sure that you do it all in one go. Many entrepreneurs use the so-called 'salami tactic', which involves firing people in different 'slices' or waves. This only causes unrest throughout the entire workforce. 'Will there be more dismissals?' 'Will I be one of them?' This is bad for staff morale. Moreover, this tactic also damages your own credibility, especially if you say that every slice is going to be the last one.

- Make sure you do the dismissal in person. This is not a task to delegate to someone else. At difficult moments, you need to demonstrate that you are the head of the company. It shows little appreciation and respect for the person concerned if you give this delicate task to someone less senior than yourself. Once again, this would damage your own credibility and authority: nobody respects a boss who hides behind others when something difficult must be done.

- Rehearse the dismissal conversation beforehand in your head. Good preparation is crucial. I know of entrepreneurs who have dismissed people over their car phone, as they travel from one meeting to another. This shows a total lack of respect for the person being fired, whose life you are about to turn upside down. Instead, carry out the conversation in a quiet and private location. Come straight to the point and don't try to sweeten the pill.

The person on the other side of the table usually has a good idea of what is going to happen and will not be interested in some preliminary chitchat or a few meaningless platitudes. Explain your decision and justify it fully.

- Plan sufficient time for the dismissal conversation. After you have broken the bad news, a period of silence often follows. It is normal that people need a few minutes to let the news sink in. When they are ready, take the time to listen to what they have to say. Answer their questions and be aware that a number of frustrations may come to the surface. Be tolerant in your response to these frustrations, without allowing the conversation to degenerate into a shouting match. Try to put yourself in the other person's position. Empathy is crucial in this kind of delicate conversation.

- Always stand by your decision and never change your mind. Also accept full responsibility for the decision and do not try to put the 'blame' on someone else. Be open and honest. You might want to try and soften the blow by saying things like 'it will all work out in the end' or 'I'm sure you will soon find a new job', but people on the receiving end find little comfort in this kind of hollow cliché.

- Once the axe has fallen, try to get things over and done with as quickly as possible. When I fire people, I usually let them leave the company the same day. I don't expect them to work a notice period. This means having all the necessary paperwork ready before the dismissal conversation. Make clear and unambiguous agreements about what must happen afterwards, including the necessary handover of work and information to other colleagues. You can't expect people to work with motivation after they have been fired. If you force them to stay for an extra month or two, this can only lead to frustration, gossip and uncomfortable situations that it is in everyone's interest to avoid. Moreover, letting people go immediately shows respect on your part by giving the person the opportunity to find a new job as quickly as possible.

- Another useful tip: I usually let dismissed employees keep their company laptop and/or smartphone. These devices are already largely written off, but they can make a big difference to the people concerned, since it is often the only computer or phone they own. As a result, it is a gesture that is much appreciated and it allows people to leave the company with at least one happy memory. In addition, I always agree to provide a written reference. This shows that you have valued their work over the years, irrespective of the circumstances of their departure. No hard feelings.

- Every dismissal has an impact on the company and certainly on the team in which the dismissed person worked. Allow no room for gossip, rumor and speculation. To avoid unnecessary unrest, communicate quickly and clearly about every dismissal. Explain why it was necessary and frame it within the broader context of the company's development. Don't forget to thank the employee(s) concerned. Once again, do not delegate these matters but communicate them personally. This is the kind of moment when employees expect to see their boss step up to the plate.

- I have no problem if people who left the company later realize that the grass isn't always greener elsewhere and wish to return. Many companies would slam the door in their face, out of spite, whereas I welcome them with open arms. It is actually a good sign for our company that they want to come back. What's more, they will be doubly motivated to try and get back on the boss's and their colleagues' good side.

For the vast majority of entrepreneurs, the need to fire people is one of the most unpleasant aspects of their work. After all, entrepreneurs are people, too! But never forget that a dismissal is always much harder for the person on the receiving end. So have pity for them – and not for yourself.

43 From the moaners to the passionate: eight types of employees

'Culture eats strategy for breakfast.' I am not usually a fan of this kind of aphorism; often, they are no more than hollow slogans. But this one hits the nail on the head. Companies in growth often overfixate on strategy at the expense of neglecting their culture. But on the road to success culture is by far the more important of the two.

A company culture is a kind of collective programming of the mind, which distinguishes one group of people from another. This culture sits inside your people's heads and determines their opinions and behavior in the workplace.

In order to forge a strong culture, you need to select your people carefully and mould them into a team. Through a process of trial and error, I have learned that there are different types of employees, each with their own form of engagement (or lack of it). Over the years, I have identified eight types

1   The **moaners and whiners** spend most of their time complaining. Nothing is as it should be: their salary and bonuses are too low, their company car is not big enough, the office coffee tastes like mud, etc. This is also the type of employee who constantly says that he/she will be leaving the company but is still there thirty years later. They are energy vampires, sucking the vitality out of the company, and they have a negative impact on their colleagues. The moaners and whiners are a cancer that makes your company sick and constantly puts the brake on its growth.

2   The **conformists** are the 'tick the box' employees. They will always do exactly what is expected of them. No less, but also no more. They follow the rules to the letter and go home each evening precisely 7 hours and 36 minutes after they arrived. They know their 'rights' in detail and make sure that their employer knows it, too – repeatedly.

3   The **opportunists** are not really committed to your company. They are only interested in making a career for themselves and see their current job – and probably your company – as a springboard to the next one. They don't really identify with your values but are constantly trying to attract the attention

of senior management in the hopes of climbing further up the ladder. They have no qualms about taking credit for the work of others.

4 The **boycotters** have just one aim: to prevent their colleagues from being successful. As a result, they are your company's saboteurs, cunning and resourceful when it comes to making things go wrong. Their philosophy is: 'If the shit hits the fan, so be it!' They will certainly do nothing to prevent this from happening. On the contrary, they kick on conflict.

5 The **'don't care'** employees will not actively obstruct or sabotage your activities, but nor will they do much to move them forward. Their job is just that: a job, and nothing more. They don't care if the company is doing well or badly. All that counts is the paycheck at the end of each month.

6 The **rebels** inject creativity into your company. They offer different and surprising angles of approach that can break open any discussion. They question everything and always want to try something new. You can't staff your company entirely with rebels, because they are chaotic and sometimes make things difficult, even when they don't have to be. That being said, you always need a few of them, because it is the rebels who challenge other employees and make them more creative.

7 The **engaged** employees are solid and reliable. The more of them you have, the better your company will be. However, they are not the same as your most passionate employees. Engaged employees rise to the level of their talent and then stop. They are satisfied with what they have achieved and have no further ambitions.

8 The **passionate** employees take things a stage further. They are constantly pushing their own boundaries and always want to exceed their own expectations. They identify strongly with the company and their personal growth goes hand in hand with its growth. These are the employees who are prepared to take risks and 'go the extra mile'. As such, they are the heart of every company. You can never employ too many of them.

Make sure that you recruit the right kind of people for your organization. Above all, be on the lookout for those with passion. If you can find them on the labor market, fine. If not, remember that a strong culture can convert engaged employees into passionate ones. In other words, a culture that gives them the necessary energy and space to grow.

Nowadays, I can nearly always tell during interviews which candidates are engaged and which ones are passionate. Call it a gut feeling. However, when I was a young and inexperienced entrepreneur, I knew too little about the different categories I have mentioned before. Often, it was only after a time that I found out what kind of people I had taken on. A conformist only reveals his true colors after months or even years. And even a boycotter may seem like a conformist at first; it is only later that he will begin his subtle acts of sabotage.

What's more, even when I did finally know what type of people I was dealing with, in many cases I waited too long before taking action. You should never have patience with moaners, boycotters, and opportunists, because they can poison your entire company culture.

Good leadership is essential to hone an effective culture. Leadership not based on titles or position within the company, but on honestly earned trust and respect. In my experience, it is usually the founders that have the biggest influence on a company's culture. A CEO, and certainly a CEO appointed from outside, might have an idea in his or her head about how the company should look and be run, but this is not the same as the vision of a founder, whose convictions come from the heart rather than the mind.

New investors often have a tendency to replace a company's founder with an external CEO. But this kind of 'temporary' outside appointee will never sense the essence of the culture – and therefore never defend that culture – as well as the founder will. So don't let those early years of indecision fool you. You, the founder, are the heart of your company.

It is the strength of your convictions, embedded in the company's DNA, that allows people to surpass themselves, turning the engaged into the passionate and the passionate into the true high-flyers that can take your organization to the next level.

Dear optimist, pessimist, and realist — while you guys were busy arguing about the glass of wine, I drank it! Sincerely, the opportunist!

– Lori Greiner

44   Every disadvantage has its advantage

Ask young entrepreneurs about their heroes and nine times out of ten you will hear that Steve Jobs or Elon Musk are their shining examples. But not in my case. My hero is Brian Acton, an American computer programmer with a fascinating life story. The name doesn't ring any bells? Don't worry; ninety-nine percent of all entrepreneurs will never have heard of him either!

Brian Acton was the forty-fourth employee at Yahoo. He earned a pile of money at the former internet giant, which was eventually destined to lose its battle for supremacy with Google. During the crazy dot.com years of the 1990s, Acton invested his cash in different internet companies. When the dot.com bubble burst around the turn of the century, he lost almost everything.

In 2007, Acton left Yahoo. He traveled the world and for many months focused his considerable talents on 'ultimate frisbee', a curious mix of frisbee, netball, basketball and American football. In 2009, he hoped to get a new job at Twitter, but was passed over for the position. He shared the news of this failure on the medium that had rejected him: 'Got denied by Twitter HQ. That's OK. It would have been a long commute.' He tried Facebook next, but with an equal lack of success.

Later that same year, Acton was one of the co-founders of WhatsApp. The early years were anything but a walk in the park. The app kept on crashing and most of the other founders were ready to throw in the towel. It was Acton who persuaded them to carry on. A crucial corner had been turned and the rest, as they say, is history. In 2014, WhatsApp was sold for a spectacular 21 billion dollars to … Facebook.

It is perhaps simplifying things a bit, but if Facebook had recruited Acton in 2009 and let him do his thing, Mark Zuckerberg could have saved himself 21 billion dollars.

Others might crow at scoring a victory of this scale and rub Zuckerberg's nose in it. But not Brian Acton. His philosophical tweets reveal his approach to life. No regrets, because regrets never get you anywhere. If you suffer rejection or a setback, just put it behind you and move on. Never give in. Life is ten percent what happens to you and ninety percent how you react to it.

In my own career as an entrepreneur, I have also shared the Acton philosophy. Rejection and setbacks have never broken my resolve; on the contrary, they simply made me stronger and more determined.

At the bank where I worked as a young man, I quickly rose through the ranks. As one of the youngest people ever in the company, I was allowed to take part in a training program for possible future directors. This program ended with an exam. You were given a question and half an hour to prepare your answer, just like in an oral exam at university. When your half hour was up, you had to defend your answer in front of a jury.

Everyone following the program knew that this test was coming and tried to prepare as thoroughly as possible by talking to as many people in the bank as possible. For some of the candidates, this preparation started more than a year in advance. After all, it was an opportunity that would send the successful candidate's career into overdrive.

Of course, when I say 'everyone', I mean everyone but me. I was working in the United States during this period and had almost no time to prepare. Instead, I was earning money for the bank. I assumed that my superiors would regard this as more important. When the exam came, I was given a question about the strategy of one of the bank's more obscure departments. In my job, I had little or no contact with this department and I had had no chance to talk with any of my colleagues about it. In short, I didn't have the faintest idea about their strategy. Not surprisingly, the exam was a fiasco.

Not that I was unduly bothered. Unlike others might have done, I did not crawl into a corner to hide or feel sorry for myself. I saw the failed exam as an opportunity to start doing other things. In particular, I saw the possibilities opening up in the slowly blossoming world of electronic payments, and so I founded Clear2Pay. Would I have done it if I had been successful in the exam? Who can say?

As with Acton at WhatsApp, the early years were often very hard going. When I visited banks to explain my idea, I could often see my conversation partners struggling to keep the smirk off their face. On a few occasions, they even showed me the door – politely, but firmly. Yet each new rejection simply served to strengthen my determination to succeed. During the next visit, I would explain myself better and with even more conviction. And in the end, of course, it worked.

As Johan Cruijff once so brilliantly put it: 'Every disadvantage has its advantage.' Hundreds of entrepreneurs have turned this simple footballer's philosophy into their own successful business philosophy. And I was one of them.

45 Senna

Entrepreneurs take risks. There is no way to avoid it. They must always be carefully considered, calculated risks and you must always plan for a worst case scenario. Yet even then, you simply cannot predict the unpredictable. Sometimes things happen that no one saw coming, so that everyone is surprised. Like COVID-19 and the subsequent crisis that has swept the world at lightning speed.

The coronavirus crisis made me think back to another crisis, now more than a decade ago. In 2008, the Lehman Brothers bank went bust. The American banking authorities refused to intervene, initiating a domino effect that brought the entire financial system to its knees. Nobody had ever imagined that this system could just implode and implode so completely. But it did. Markets were frozen and bank after bank, many of them leading names, stood on the point of collapse. The level of distrust between the financial institutions grew to unprecedented heights, so that no one was prepared to lend money to anyone else. The world economy ground to a halt.

Clear2Pay was in the eye of the storm. Our main activity was the sale of software to banks. These banks were notoriously slow payers. But at least you knew they would always pay in the end, even if it usually took 120 days. During the crisis, this changed. The banks now informed us that they were currently no longer able to pay their outstanding accounts: all their liquid assets were blocked in the financial system. Some of them even refused to sign future order forms. 120 days became more than 240 days.

I can remember that period as if it was yesterday. It was a nightmare. We needed to pay something like three million euros each month in wages, but had almost no cash coming in. No matter how hard we pressed them, the banks refused to settle their accounts.

It was an absurd and extremely frustrating situation. If you default on a loan repayment with a bank, the penalty clauses (with interest) start mounting up with immediate effect and every second day you get a new legal letter threatening you with this or that dire consequence. But if the banks default on their payments? Nothing. Nada. Their basic principle is: 'My problem is always your problem, but your problem is never mine.'

Fortunately, at the eleventh hour the government intervened to save the banks and payments began to flow through the system once more. We were also fortunate that our own suppliers, aware of the problem, were willing to wait for their money from us until the banks had coughed up. Even so, it had been a close call.

If the situation had lasted for another month, we would have had no option but to file for bankruptcy. And then I would never have written a book. Unless it was a very different kind of book. The margin between success and failure is often very small; much smaller than many entrepreneurs think.

The events of 2008 brought home to us the grim reality of the risks that entrepreneurs sometimes need to deal with. We had to invest all our private resources back into the company just to pay the wages and keep our heads barely above water.

We each paid according to our ability, but it was my partner Michel Akkermans who financed the lion's share. I had nothing left in my bank account. For me, it was a question of all or nothing. I remember telling my wife that it was going to be touch and go. If we could pull through, everything would be all right. But if we went under, we would lose everything we had, including the company. I slept badly for months on end and felt stressed out all the time. My hair was already greying before the financial crisis. By the time it finished, I was completely grey.

It was during this period that I learned that you always need to take account of the possible effect of unforeseen circumstances. You need to be prepared for even the most unlikely scenarios. With this in mind, it is a good idea for every company to organize a kind of 'stress test' at least once each year, to simulate the kind of impact that an unexpected crisis could have on your company. In this way, you will be better able to respond if a crisis breaks in real life.

Whereas the financial crisis of 2008 hit the financial sector hardest, the impact of the COVID-19 crisis of 2020 is far more wide-ranging. In just a few months, large sectors of the economy were reduced from one hundred percent activity to zero percent. Many companies were forced to close down.

In this kind of situation, the key is to respond as efficiently and effectively as possible. Don't panic and keep a cool head. Of course, there needs to be a sense of urgency. But while some experienced companies developed and implemented an emergency rescue plan in a matter of days, in some cases turning their business model upside down, I saw many other companies do nothing. Head in the sand, hoping that the storm would pass and leave them untouched. Wishful thinking.

That is not the way the world works. In a crisis you must have the courage to take hard decisions and radically cut your costs. Okay, 'you can't shrink yourself into greatness', as the saying goes. But in a crisis it is not about greatness; it is about survival – and doing nothing is no strategy at all. This is something I experienced first hand in 2008: if I had not insisted immediately on prompt cost-cutting action, Clear2Pay would not have survived long enough to benefit from the state bailout.

Another much-heard business saying is 'Never waste a good crisis.' There is an important element of truth in this. A crisis often has a beneficial effect in the long run. It teaches entrepreneurs to question the status quo and to assess whether their current way of working is actually the best way. Perhaps yesterday's 'recipes for success' will no longer provide the future growth of tomorrow. A crisis also has a kind of Darwinian effect on the economy. The weak wither and die and only the fittest companies survive. This is tragic for those who don't make it, since each bankruptcy has a painful human cost, but it is a typical – and necessary – feature of a healthy economy.

The legendary Formula 1 driver, the late, great Ayrton Senna, was a past master at racing in poor conditions. It is one of things that helped to make him a triple world champion. If it was raining, the Brazilian was not just a little bit better than his rivals; he humiliated them. When the rain started to fall, other drivers froze with stress, but not Senna. His confidence grew because he knew that in these conditions he was seconds per lap faster than anyone else. During interviews, he explained with great panache that it was much easier to overtake fifteen other drivers when it was raining than when the sun was shining.

The best entrepreneurs also have a touch of this Senna magic. During a crisis, they do not hesitate or try to hide, but have the guts to press their foot down on the gas pedal even harder. These are the moments when a real difference can be made. It is not only Formula 1 drivers who need to adapt to the twists and turns of the circuit; maneuverability when times are tough is also an all-important quality for every entrepreneur.

46 Double whammy

I always encourage companies to move into foreign markets as soon as possible. As countries go, Belgium is only the size of a large handkerchief, so that upscaling and growth almost by definition involve internationalization. Besides, in many countries 'made in Belgium' is a much-prized quality label. Consequently, many companies will sell their products more quickly abroad than in the conservative domestic market.

Most companies try to conquer the foreign market with a fairly standard method. They rent an office somewhere and send one of their most talented people to work there. This Belgian (but it also applies to a Brit, an American, etc.) then has to put together a team of local employees to take the local market by storm.

Take it from me: this strategy does not work. You will need to burn a lot of money before the engine starts. Even if that person is a superstar in his own country, his status abroad will be zero, so he has to build up a new reputation from scratch. He doesn't know the local culture, has no network and (as a result of bad hires) will need to change his team several times in a relatively short period. He will have to take decisions quickly, but quick decisions often mean wrong decisions. It takes months to build up first-class references and you need to spend a fortune on marketing to get even just a little bit of local brand awareness.

For all these reasons, I have never used this method to grow my companies internationally. In my opinion, there is a better, faster and cheaper method: you take over a small company in your target country that already has your key target customer in its portfolio.

If you want to use this strategy, it is best to search for smaller companies that work on an exclusively local basis and do not (yet) have any international activities. They should operate at break-even or make a small profit, so that they are not too expensive to acquire. The most important thing is that their products, which they only sell locally, are very good. So good, in fact, that you can sell them elsewhere in your group and find new markets for them. This is not only good for your revenue but also for the commission of your sales people, who can immediately add the products to their sales pack.

The reverse process works as well: you can sell your own products to the local customers of the company you have taken over. In this way, the sales cycle, which in normal circumstances could easily last for twelve months, can be reduced to less than six months. After all, given that there is already a relationship of trust between the local customers and the local company that you now own, this will allow you to shift your 'foreign' products more easily.

Selling your own products faster in a new international market and introducing a new international product in your domestic market: this strategy is what I call the 'double whammy'. Profit twice over. It is a 'two birds with one stone' strategy that allows you to grow much faster than companies that adopt an alternative strategy.

I first made use of the double whammy strategy at Metris. Using this method, the company made acquisitions in the United States and Germany, before going to the stock market. Likewise with Clear2Pay. We never opened foreign offices but instead took over companies in the Netherlands, France, Australia and Chile. Thanks to this strategy, in less than ten years we were able to build up an international group. If you want to achieve the same result organically, by opening your own offices, the process will take much longer.

Many entrepreneurs will tell you that taking over a foreign company is not a risk they wish to take. How will they pay for the acquisition when their own company is still relatively small? They seem to forget that shares are also a form of cash and that, consequently, they can finance the takeover in part with shares in their own company.

In this way, the company involves their managers and their existing shareholders in the adventure, so that it is in everyone's interest to make sure that the value of the shares increases.

47 M&A: from the perspective of the seller

M&A: Mergers and Acquisitions. Sooner or later, most entrepreneurs will be involved with one or the other, or both. Over the years, I have bought and sold dozens of companies.

Like raising capital from investors, buying and selling companies is an art. It is a market overflowing with cash and there are even consultants who can earn big money for advising buyers or sellers.

I would like to share a number of lessons that I learned on both sides of the negotiating table. I will start by looking at things from the perspective of the seller.

The first major lesson I discovered is that time kills deals. When you start a transaction, the buyer and the seller are both enthusiastic. During the early months, everything goes smoothly, but after a while a certain 'deal fatigue' starts to make itself felt. Negotiating day and night makes people nervous and more irritable. The engine begins to splutter and frustrations rise to the surface.

You need to try to conclude the deal before you reach this point. So make a clear plan for the negotiations and set your negotiating partner a deadline, which serves as a milestone that cannot be missed.

When you are selling a company, it is also important not to give exclusivity to a single buyer too quickly. Try to keep as many potential players in the game for as long as you can, and make sure that each player knows that there are rival candidates. This helps you to keep the price high and to limit the number of legal provisions in the contract.

Remember that selling a company puts a heavy burden on your core team. It is often the same people who need to attend all the many meetings and they must be familiar with the mountains of information that these meetings inevitably involve. At the same time, don't forget that somebody must also be available to 'mind the store'. While the management is selling the company, others need to keep it running. It cannot be allowed to stand still or stagnate and its sale cannot be an excuse for failing to reach the figures for the coming quarters. If this happens, the buyer will be quick to take advantage of the situation to force down the takeover price. So make sure that your sales, operations, and financial reporting are all maintained at their target levels throughout the transaction.

This is one of the classic mistakes made by inexperienced entrepreneurs. Usually, a CFO will need to spend about sixty percent of his time on the transaction, whereas for the CEO and the COO this figure rises to roughly eighty percent. In young companies, where there are always a thousand-and-one things to do and not all that many people to do them, this can have a serious negative effect on the normal running of the company.

For this reason, it is never too early to start preparing for your company's sale. It is even a good idea to start before you have even seriously thought about selling. In all the companies in which I have been involved (and as I mentioned in the chapter on raising capital), I set up an exit committee from the very first day. When you are ready to move on to the next phase of your entrepreneurial adventure, you will be glad that you made this decision.

The exit committee is a subset of the board of directors and the senior managers. It usually meets twice a year to discuss and document various matters of interest. Who are our competitors? How are we different from them? What other companies might be interested in purchasing ours? What is the value of our company and how do we determine this figure?

Put simply, the exit committee must make the company ready for sale. Is there a data room in the cloud? Are all our policy documents in order? Do we have the necessary contacts with investment bankers and analysts?

If you think in good time about a potential exit, you won't be taken by surprise if you suddenly receive a takeover bid. Arriving at the negotiating table well prepared puts you in a strong position to dominate the proceedings.

When you are selling, it is also important not to lose sight of your workforce. The final contract will probably include (financial) provisions on paper for the senior management. Try to secure similar arrangements for your other people. For example, you can set aside a specified amount that will be shared out to the employees who are still active in the company three years after its takeover.

I have often noticed how during negotiations people have a tendency to think first and foremost about themselves and forget that many others have contributed to the success of the company over the years, without which it would not be such an attractive takeover proposition. It is a cliché but money does indeed do strange things to people.

One of the more technical aspects of a takeover relates to the issue of open source. If your company makes software, it is possible that your programmers have made use of open source material in the coding of their programs. Open source software is software that you can download from the web, the source code of which you can then adjust to suit your specific needs. Programmers use open source elements so that they can write their own codes more quickly.

Companies often do not have the faintest idea which of these open source elements have been included in their proprietary software. American companies ask this information as standard wherever they are considering a takeover. If you do not have the necessary summary to hand over, this can slow down the transaction procedure, as well as costing a lot of money to have all your software re-analyzed. It would be a great shame if this was the cause of your deal falling through.

When you finally decide to sell your company, you can either opt for the 'locked box' method or for the 'closing accounts' method. The 'locked box' method takes as its basis the most recent account balance and results. The buyer and seller agree on a price and also set adjusted levels for the working capital, the net debt, etc. From that moment on, the price remains fixed and the balance and all related figures are frozen. This is also the moment when both the economic risk and any subsequent benefits are transferred from the seller to the buyer.

With the 'closing accounts' method, a provisional price for the takeover is agreed, based on the estimated figures for working capital, net debts, etc. The buyer and the seller also agree on a date when the deal will be 'closed' and at that moment adjust the provisional price on the basis of the actual figures. This method frequently gives rise to more discussion.

Another important aspect in any takeover is the need to draw up the best possible term sheet. This contains all the different provisions and definitions relating to the takeover, such as price, conditions, timings, etc. The more details you can include in the term sheet, the easier it will be to make the transition from the sheet to the final contract, since you will have fewer discussions as you approach the end of your negotiations. And fewer discussions is good for all concerned!

Often, conditions are mentioned in the takeover contract that each party must satisfy before the deal can actually be regarded as completed. These are the so-called closing conditions. Be extremely careful what you agree to. Sometimes these conditions can seriously delay the prompt conclusion of the takeover, which can cost you a lot of money.

A classic in this respect is the condition that all your employees must sign a non-competition agreement. If this provision is not standard in your contract of employment, this means that you have to arrange for all your people to sign a separate new agreement. Sometimes they will refuse, in the hope that they can negotiate a higher bonus before the company is sold. Not really fair, perhaps, but it does happen. Closing conditions might seem like details on paper, but in reality they can seriously complicate your deal in extremis.

That being said, having a non-competition agreement is generally a good idea. Once when we were taking over a company, we asked the seller to arrange for all his employees to sign such an agreement. The sales staff were not happy with this and after long discussions we agreed to a limited list of signatories, omitting employees who were regarded as 'non-crucial'. We soon found out that this was a big mistake. Less than a month after the takeover, some of these non-crucial employees set up a rival company of their own. We couldn't stop them, because they hadn't signed a non-competition agreement. It cost our company a lot of lost time and even more money.

Also be careful with future projections. Sellers often try to 'optimize' their figures in the hope of getting a better price. They keep their anticipated costs low and give their future revenue a serious boost. But if the negotiations for the deal drag on much longer than you anticipated, this is a strategy that can boomerang in your face if these projected figures are not met.

Immediately before the final conclusion of any deal, I always compare the projected figures with the actual figures. There is often a significant difference, because the seller was over-optimistic in his assessment. As the buyer, I can use this to try to get something extra knocked off the price at the last minute.

By this stage, it is usually too late for the seller to just walk away from the deal. They have already planned what they want to do with the money and so they have little option other than to (very reluctantly) drop their asking price. But it serves them right for trying to massage their figures!

Of course, no deal is ever truly completed until the money is credited to your bank account. I have often been involved in deals that fell through at the very last moment. As our American friends like to say: 'It ain't over till it's over'.

48 M&A: from the perspective of the buyer

In an earlier chapter, I talked about the double whammy strategy. Taking over companies abroad is a good way to encourage rapid international growth. Of course, that is easier said than done. Concluding a successful takeover is by no means easy and it is not a matter that you should take lightly.

It is a good idea to set up a separate team that is responsible for all your takeovers. This team must also handle the integrational and operational aspects of the deal for a period of twelve months after a takeover has taken place. This allows you to avoid the situation where one team concludes the deal and another team implements it, which is a perfect scenario for passing the buck if the integration does not go as smoothly as planned.

I have concluded many takeovers and acted as an adviser in plenty of others. A successful takeover usually depends on making the best possible analysis of the company you want to acquire. I always draw up a memorandum that covers the reasons for the takeover, the financial projections, and the valuations on which these are based. To this I add a SWOT analysis, a summary of the cost savings that can be achieved through integration, a worst case scenario, and a description of the team.

I am amazed that many companies still fail to compile this kind of memorandum when they are considering a takeover. This means that they are planning to spend millions on a company that they don't really know! The memorandum also has a subsidiary internal benefit: it makes it possible to remind 'forgetful' managers about their part in the takeover process, since their signature will also be on the memorandum document (which is something I insist on).

If you are responsible for conducting a takeover, try to avoid so-called 'fly-in' behavior. Sometimes, the management team of the prospective buyer will try to show just how important they are by all jumping on a plane to visit the target company en masse. Like a flock of seagulls, they descend on the company's various departments, leaving behind little bits of shit everywhere, before flying off again just as suddenly as they arrived. This totally confuses the local team, who have no idea what to make of all the different (and often wholly contradictory) signals they have received. Believe me, it is not the best way to start important negotiations. So keep your managers where they belong: with their feet firmly on the ground.

In every takeover contract there is mention of 'reps' and 'warranties'. These are legal clauses that govern certain conditions of the deal. You can deviate from these conditions via so-called 'disclosures': provisions that allow exceptions to be made to the reps (which stands for representations), for which the buyer can never claim compensation, since everything has been agreed beforehand.

Imagine, for example, that a rep stipulates that the selling company should no longer pay out any bonuses, but a member of staff nevertheless receives a bonus after the transaction date. This exception must be mentioned in the disclosures. If it is not, the buyer will have the right to deduct the amount of the bonus from the acquisition price. This shows that disclosures need to be taken seriously and it pays to re-examine all the disclosures, reps and warranties six months or a year later, just to make sure that everyone has stuck to the agreed rules. In this way, you can avoid unpleasant (and often expensive) surprises.

If I make a financial projection, I always take account of the unwritten business law that says that revenue will decrease after a takeover. The first quarter after the deal has been concluded is always bad and always displays the same pattern: revenue falls by at least twenty-five percent and only recovers to its original level after three further quarters, before then continuing to rise.

I have forgotten the number of takeover deals I have been involved in, but I know for certain that this pattern was evident in every one of them. Is it because the transaction took too long? Or is it the result of a lack of focus by management during the transaction negotiations? I have no idea! But no matter what the seller says should happen, I always include this revenue dip in my calculations. Otherwise, it is not at lot of fun having to go to your board of directors so soon after the takeover to ask for more money!

I have also learned that the real work only begins after the takeover has taken place. Buying a new company is not difficult; integrating it successfully into your existing setup is something else entirely. For this reason, I always add an extra provision to the budget over and above the acquisition price, to cover the costs of an effective integration process. Most companies fail to do this, so that the integration runs into difficulties that are even more costly in the long run.

Part of the problem is that managers are not willing to bear the integration costs if the costs need to be covered by their own budget. But if there is a separate budget, that is a different matter.

A final piece of advice that I would like to share is this: be on your guard against the possible effects of the so-called 'earn-out' mechanism. With an earn-out, part of the acquisition price is dependent on the future performance of the company. A number of predetermined parameters, such as revenue or other key milestones, are measured over a certain period and converted into a valuation formula. Since any earn-out compensation is only paid later on, it can be taken out of the company's cash flow.

Even so, I am not a big fan of earn-outs. They are complex and give rise to discussion. It is easy for the buyer to manipulate the figures; for example, by increasing costs or by deferring revenue. To avoid this, sellers usually ask for guarantees that the senior management of the buyer company will not change the rules relating to the operational running of the company during the earn-out period. However, this is not, in my opinion, a healthy situation. You buy a company precisely with the intention of running it and integrating it into your operations. Not being able to so during this crucial first period is the very last thing you want, particularly if things turn out badly. Often, the only solution is to pay the full earn-out to the seller.

In other words, the earn-out-mechanism prevents you from taking control of your new company from the first day of your ownership. This is contrary to what entrepreneurship is all about. For this reason, I never agree to it.

Wall Street is the only place that people ride to in a Rolls Royce to get advice from those who take the subway.

– Warren Buffett

49   All work and no play ...

Entrepreneurship can be demanding. Hard work, long hours, tons of stress at crucial moments – and it all falls on your shoulders, even if you have an excellent team. What's more, in the world of entrepreneurship, pressure to perform, egotism, greed, and envy are never far away. I have always been aware of the dangers of being under the gun for prolonged periods. As a result, I make sure that I have regular periods of relaxation and decompression.

An entrepreneur needs to have a safety valve. It is good for him or her to let off steam every now and then. Occasionally, I just need to get away from it all and do something else. Preferably something fun. Playing practical jokes. Fooling people. Basically, acting like a big kid. This is what works for me. It helps me to escape from that 'other' world, where everything is so serious.

In particular, I can remember one such moment in Sydney, a city where jet lag makes working brutal, even under the best of circumstances. We were there to negotiate our first big contract for Clear2Pay. With this kind of deal, the round-table sessions regularly last for up to twelve hours. Hundreds of pages need to be reviewed; there are discussions over almost every word; sometimes even over commas and full stops. This is not good for your jet-lagged body and mind! One of our team actually fell fast asleep at a crucial point during the final meeting!

Even so, after three days and nights of hell, we finally had our deal. It was a real milestone for our young company, something that deserved to be celebrated. Michel and I had already developed the (admittedly childish) habit of taking turns to try to convince people we met in bars of the craziest things. Our stories kept getting more and more fanciful. We were Jehovah's Witnesses. We were secret agents. We were astronauts. You get the idea. Whichever of us was first unmasked as an impostor lost the game. Selling nonsense to the point of credibility: it is a pastime that you can enjoy anywhere in the world – and it is not bad practice for an entrepreneur!

In Sydney, we got into conversation with two nurses from Manchester. When they asked what had brought us from Belgium to Australia, Michel instantly replied that we were undertakers! The game was on! I told the girls that that we were specialized in the repatriation of rich businessmen who died abroad.

As the game demanded, Michel kept on piling improbability upon improbability. He explained that our service was unique, because during the flight home we ensured that the deceased's coffin was always turned to point in the direction of the sun. I added that this ritual was performed in a swimming pool we had specially installed in our plane.

By this time, we were finding it hard to contain our laughter and the nurses were starting to catch on to what we were doing. 'You're making fun of us!' they said. I thought the game was up, but Michel had the ultimate trump card up his sleeve. He opened his wallet and pulled out a business card from his former company: FICS. 'Funeral InCorporated Services,' he explained with a deadpan face.

There was no way I could top that, so I graciously conceded defeat. This time Michel had won. Happily, the nurses could also see the funny side of things and we spent a great evening together.

Another moment that I won't forget in a hurry was a particular first of April at Clear2Pay. April Fool's Day. We told everyone in the company that we had decided to change our name. We had been around for quite a while and things were going well; so much so that we were now a well-established player in the financial world. As a result, we thought the time had come to change the name from Clear2Pay to Here2Stay! We had even made a false website, false visitors cards, etc. to convince them! I can still see the looks of disbelief on their faces. Priceless!

Perhaps you think that we put too much time, effort and money into a silly April Fool's joke? Perhaps we did, but during an unbelievably busy period it did us a huge amount of good simply to let off some steam and have a bit of a laugh. Entrepreneurship has to be something more than work, work, work; otherwise, you will never last the course.

50 Sitting is the new smoking

As a student, I always preferred to walk around while I was studying. During the exam period, I must have done hundreds if not thousands of laps of our back garden, book in hand. And as my total number of kilometers grew, so I eventually came to sense exactly the right pace to achieve the best effect. Not too slow. Not too fast. Just the right speed to fix everything I needed to know in my head.

Our ancient ancestors used to cover huge distances on foot. They had no choice, if they wanted to find food. According to historians, they probably walked an average of thirty kilometers a day!

Until the start of the 20th century, working on the land was the main economic activity for a large part of the population. They didn't need to think about the importance of physical exercise. They got plenty of it every day in the fields and woods. This is no longer the case for us today – and it is an evolution that is gathering speed all the time.

When I was a kid, I was always outside. In my free time, I played football, climbed trees and generally romped around. This has now all changed, in just a single generation. Modern teenagers – I have some at home, so I know what I am talking about – now spend most of the day glued to a screen (computer or smartphone, it doesn't matter which), playing cool games with their equally cool friends.

But it is not just the teenagers who have lost the habit of movement. We adults also spend an average of nine hours a day sitting down. In other words, more than a third of each day. Add to that the hours of sleep and there isn't much time left over for physical activity of any kind.

When I began to work at the bank fulltime after graduating, walking soon disappeared from my life. I got up, ate breakfast and joined the morning traffic jam for the hour-long journey from Antwerp to Brussels, where I spent the next ten hours in an office. The only exercise I had was the few hundred meters between the office and our lunchtime cafeteria. At the end of the day, it was another hour of traffic to get home, followed by an evening meal and two or three hours in front of the television. This seated existence soon had an effect on me. My mood worsened and my weight increased. Within a couple of years, I had put on ten kilos.

Just in time, I read a few interesting books on sleep, diet and exercise, and their impact on our health. This gave me the wake-up call I needed. I learned that people who sit too much have an increased risk of cardiovascular disease, diabetes and cancer. And people who sit for eleven hours a day have forty percent more chance of dying young than people who only sit for four hours a day. Little wonder that sitting is now regarded by many as the new smoking. And, to a large extent, they are not wrong.

I often hear entrepreneurs say that they have no time to exercise. True, it can sometimes be difficult to find a spare half hour or so. Even so, I now organize my days so that I still do enough physical activity to keep me fit.

For example, twenty years ago I bought myself a home trainer and I try to cycle at least twenty kilometers each day. I do these kilometers while I am watching the news on TV or sometimes while reading through a business plan. In this way, I can mix work and sport in a fun way. Although at first, as with walking in my student days, it took me some time to find the best speed for combining cycling and reading!

A simple adjustment that can also make a huge difference is to always take the stairs instead of using the lift. With this in mind, many companies now stick tape on the floor, pointing in the direction of the stairs – and it works. Standing offices also help to occasionally break the monotony of the sitting routine.

Walking meetings are another great idea. Steve Jobs used to love them and much preferred a meeting on the move to a meeting in a conference room. Not only do they get you away from the daily office grind, but it has also been proven that our brains work better when we are moving. Walking stimulates our creativity. Just try it! After a walking meeting you will have fresh ideas and new insights.

Companies that allow and encourage their employees to exercise during office hours are rewarded with a happier and more productive workforce. The few 'lost' hours for sport are more than compensated for by greater enthusiasm and efficiency.

Make your people aware of the dangers of not getting enough exercise. I have given many of my colleagues a book by Tom Rath: *Eat Move Sleep*. The author was told at an early age that he had a rare disease and would not live many more years.

He decided to change his lifestyle completely and began to eat, exercise and sleep in a totally different way. I re-read Rath's inspirational guide at least once a year and would recommend everyone to do the same.

What I thought would make me productive

What actually makes me productive

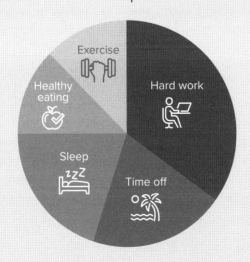

Conclusion

Because I am an eternal optimist, I seriously underestimated what this book project would involve. Which is perhaps just as well – otherwise I might never have started. I wrote most of the chapters while sitting on a plane, traveling from one business meeting to another. It has taken me quite a long while to complete, but I truly enjoyed the process: looking back at my own entrepreneurial adventures, thinking about the lessons I could pass on to today's budding entrepreneurs, and looking forward to what the future still holds in store for me.

During the writing of the book, I became more aware than ever that I am someone who is always on the search for something new. I need constant stimulation and like nothing better than to have many irons in the fire. That can be tiring, not only for me, but also for the people around me. Even so, it makes for a life that is fascinating and full. Never a dull moment. I am no longer as young as I once was, but my quest for new challenges continues.

Is that, perhaps, the secret of a successful entrepreneur? That you need to be a restless soul? Non-stop searching inspires creativity and that is the fundamental quality that every entrepreneur must possess if he or she hopes to be successful.

What many entrepreneurs lose sight of (or at least fail to share sufficiently with others) is the fact that entrepreneurship is, first and foremost, fun. But if you don't want to lose the necessary passion and drive, it is essential to strike the right balance, both at work and at home. Make clear agreements. Give quality time with your family the same importance you attach to a crucial business meeting. Both must be something you would never cancel.

Take good care of yourself. Exercise and a healthy lifestyle are important weapons against stress.

Being an entrepreneur can be lonely. For this reason, throughout my career I have deliberately sought out mentors, experienced entrepreneurs who had already walked the road that I hoped to follow. Entrepreneurs who could inspire and help me. Above all, surround yourself with positive people.

Many people have helped me in my entrepreneurial journey, but many others have consciously tried to hinder me. The business world is a competitive one; there are always sharks nearby. When money is involved, people do strange things. For this reason, entrepreneurs must avoid being naïve. Don't get taken in by the first tempting partnership that you are offered and don't let others attach their wagon to your star, unless it is in your interests as well.

The best evidence that you are on the right track as an entrepreneur is your customers. If they are willing to pay for your product and service, your company is in a good place. Listen to your customers and cherish them. Far too many entrepreneurs are constantly in search of new customers, so that they sometimes forget that their real capital is in their existing customers. It costs far less time and money to keep an existing customer on board than to attract a new one.

I hope that this book will stimulate some of my readers to live their own entrepreneurial dream. It is never too late to start. I am convinced that in the future we will need more entrepreneurs, if we wish to maintain our current levels of prosperity. Entrepreneurship can be hard, but there is nothing finer than being your own boss, implementing your own ideas and creating your own company from scratch. If you have been bitten by the entrepreneurial bug, don't hesitate: just go for it. Let nothing or no one stand in your way.

There are a few people I would like to thank in particular. First and foremost, my wife Sarie, for her years of constant support. Also my parents, for a loving home and a fine upbringing. I encourage my children Timon and Fien to first read this book, if they ever consider becoming entrepreneurs. Above all, they must do what they want to do and follow what their heart tells them. After all, that is what I have always done.

I could never have completed this book without the help of others. My thanks go to Jeroen, who has guided me through this adventure and corrected my many spelling mistakes. And to my personal assistant Julie, for her daily support in everything that I do, and to Vince for his refinements American-style. Last but not least, a big thank you Bert, Machteld, Charlotte, Elly, Sally and Leen for reading parts of the text.

The experiences and anecdotes that I mention in the book were shared with dozens and dozens of fantastic partners, colleagues and friends. Without them, I would be neither the entrepreneur nor man that I am today. I am also grateful to my former employees at Clear2Pay for their years of unfailing effort and support. We really did it, didn't we?

Thank you all for helping me to make my dream come true.

Manna doesn't just
fall from the sky.

– Gilbert Ingels, my caring, cool, and non-entrepreneurial
  father, who died far too young

About the author

Jürgen Ingels (16 March 1971, Roeselare) is an entrepreneur and risk capitalist. He studied Political and Social Sciences at the University of Antwerp and later went on to graduate with a Master of Business Administration (MBA) degree. He started his career as an investment manager at Dexia Ventures, the risk capital fund of the Dexia banking group.

His major breakthrough came with Clear2Pay, a pioneering company in the field of financial technology that he founded in 2001 and that eventually grew into a successful international business with 1,200 employees and offices in more than twenty countries. In 2014, Clear2Pay was sold to FIS (NYSE), one of the largest fintech companies in the world. After the sale, he returned to his first love: risk capital. Today, Jürgen is a managing partner at SmartFin, a risk capital fund that invests in growing European technology companies (www.smartfinvc.com). He is also a director of various other companies, both large and small, including WDP (Euronext/BEL20), Materialise (NASDAQ), Ghelamco, Itiviti, Guardsquare, Unified Post, Deliverect and many more.

Jürgen has a huge passion for technology and entrepreneurship, and this is reflected in everything he does. These twin passions resulted in initiatives such as Supernova and The Big Score, two important Belgian technology festivals with international allure. In 2015, Jürgen was chosen as ICT Personality of the Year in Belgium.

The man from West Flanders is also well known for his appearances in the TV program *Leeuwenkuil*, which was first broadcast on VIER (Channel Four) in 2018. In this Flemish version of *Shark Tank* (USA) or *Dragons' Den* (Britain), passionate entrepreneurs – some already experienced, others just starting out – are given the opportunity to pitch their idea to five potential investors. Jürgen is still involved with a number of the companies resulting from the program.

Company X
Index list for data room

1.   Corporate information

1.1   Corporate organization charts (legal structure with subsidiaries and legal entities) showing perimeter of the transaction

1.2   Per subsidiary: full name – date and country of incorporation and registered number – total issued capital and percentage held – other shareholders (if any)

1.3   Copy of the company's articles of association as issued on the date of incorporation and as of today

1.4   Overview of all subsequent changes to the articles of association

1.5   Current shareholder structure (include copy Shareholders Register and subsidiaries) including director's interest with detailed information on the outstanding shares including

      a.   description of each class of shares

      b.   number of shares by class and face value

      c.   identity of shareholders

      d.   details of outstanding warrants/options

1.6   Details of any shareholder agreements relating to the group, any subsidiary, associate or related company

1.7   Details of any pre-emption, tag-along or drag-along rights with respect to the shares to be transferred to the purchaser

1.8   Trade register

1.9   Copies of the board minutes relating to the last 3 years and any resolution of General Meetings requiring filing

1.10   Copies of the minutes of the shareholder's meetings (last 3 years)

1.11   Milestones in the history of the group

    1.11.1   Internal growth

    1.11.2   Overview of external growth, divestments and other changes in perimeter since inception

2. **Financial and auditing**

2.1 Consolidated and individual group financial statements for the last three financial periods (P&L, balance sheet, cash flow statement)

2.2 Description of the accounting rules and changes (if any) approved during the last 5 years

2.3 Copies of last 3 years auditor's management letters with comments from the management

2.4 Copies of internal audit reports (last 3 years)

2.5 Positions since last accounts (dividends, capital commitments, material adverse change in business or prospects)

2.6 Revenues

2.6.1 Description of recurring and non-recurring revenues

2.6.2 Historical record of figures of the group's sales (last 3 years)
   a. Revenues per product / region
   b. Revenues per type of clients / for major clients
   c. Other relevant turnover split

2.6.3 Monthly revenues year-to-date

2.7 Profitability

2.7.1 Description of measurements of the profitability (EBITDA, EBIT, NPBT …) and key performance indicators used by the group

2.7.2 Historical of figures of the group's profitability (last 3 years)
   a. Profitability per product / region
   b. Revenues per type of clients / for major clients
   c. Other relevant turnover split

2.8 Costs

2.8.1 Description of cost structure

2.8.2 Cost of goods sold (Panels, Project partners)

2.8.3 Description of personnel costs (HR) (details are in Human Resources section): Insights, Data, Tech, Sales, Sales Support, HR & OPS

2.8.4 Description of SG&A costs (Travel, Marketing, Communication & IT, Rent, Legal and accounting, other)

2.8.5 Description of amortization and depreciation: detailed historic depreciation tables for the last 3 years and review of future depreciation for existing assets

2.9 Analysis of all exceptional (and extraordinary) items over the last 3 years

2.10 Analysis of interest expenses and financial revenues over the last 3 years

2.11 Consolidated Cash flow statement (including capex and working capital requirements) in the last 3 years

2.12 Balance sheet

2.12.1 Details of fixed assets (nature of both tangible and intangible fixed assets as well as financial assets)

2.12.2 Details of financial debt (ST – LT) and conditions

2.12.3 Details of outstanding financial liabilities and linked reimbursement schemes

2.12.4 Analysis of the provisions (especially expected timing of cash-out)

2.12.5 Description of any subsidies

2.12.6 Detailed description of origin, nature and estimated evolution of existing deferred tax liabilities and deferred tax assets (last 3 years)

2.12.7 Working capital elements

a. Trade receivables

- Descriptive current payment conditions
- Average client receivables turnover ratio over the last 3 years
- Ageing list (any write-offs on trade receivables)

b. Trade payables

c. Stock (any write-offs on stock, other?) or WIP (work in progress)

2.12.8 Analysis of the off-balance sheet obligations or liabilities (e.g. factoring, material collateral pledged by the company or its affiliates or guarantees or keep-well agreements)

3. Reporting, budget and business plan

3.1 Reporting system

3.1.1 Explanation of the management reporting systems and definition of the relevant groups for analytical accounting

3.1.2 Copy of the group's management accounts (last 3 years)

3.1.3 Reconciliation between the management accounts and the published P&L accounts, balance sheet and cash flow statements

3.1.4 3 years' history of:

        a. Sales by service/product (volume and value)

        b. Sales by geographic area

        c. Sales by customer

        d. Sales by distribution channel

        e. Sales concentration statistics (10% largest customers represent x% of sales)

        f. Operational KPIs

3.2   Budget and budgeting process

    3.2.1   Budget for current year and thereafter

    3.2.2   Description of forecasting process and budget procedure

    3.2.3   Management procedure on follow up of the budget

3.3   Business plan

    3.3.1   Presentation of the consolidated business plan (P&L – balance sheet – CF statement)

    3.3.2   Details of the method and basis of preparation of the forecasts and the underlying assumptions (general economic, competitive, political …) in terms of revenues and charges

4.   Business overview

4.1   Description of the strategy of the group / substantial business risks

4.2   Description of Strategic Alliances or Joint Ventures (if any)

4.3   Overview of activities of the group

4.4   Description of the value chain/process flow of the different services

4.5   Description of the production process (outsourced or internal, etc.)

5.   Market and competition

5.1   Segmentation of the market and general description per market segment

        a. Market size in volume and value

        b. Market size per geographic area

        c. Market size evolution over last 3 years and for future 5 years

        d. Description of key success factors

5.2   Market potential per service/product in each region

5.3   Competition

    5.3.1   List of most relevant competitors

    5.3.2   Competitive advantage vis-a-vis competitors

5.4   Most important co-operative or information sharing agreements with competitors in the last 5 years, if any

5.5 Overview of important national or European or US legislation/regulation having an impact on the business/market potential

5.6 SWOT analysis and specificity of the group

6. Sales and markerting

6.1 Description of client segments (to the relevant group level)

6.2 Description of the commercial strategy, main marketing activities and expenditures

6.3 Market/industry reports

6.4 Pricing policy

    6.4.1 General terms and conditions

    6.4.2 Price formation

    6.4.3 List of customers with special arrangements or extended terms

6.5 Contracts

    6.5.1 General standard terms and conditions for sales and details of guarantee services

    6.5.2 Copies of all contracts with customers for the sale of services/products in excess of 5,000 euros

    6.5.3 Details of any abnormal factor in contracts

6.6 Details of any customer complaints

6.7 Details of any loss of important clients due to an abnormal factor

6.8 Expected end of product life cycle for each of the products + new products and brand developments

7. Procurement

7.1 Description of the purchasing policy

7.2 Description of the largest purchasing accounts

7.3 Description of the top ten service/goods providers

7.4 Description of service contracts related to administration (personnel, IT, accountant, consultant …)

7.5 Description of intra-company transactions and transfer pricing policy

8. Partnership with partners and suppliers

8.1 Description of strategic partners

8.2 Description of agreements with strategic partners: exclusivity, price/discount, etc.

8.3 Details of potential problems with strategic partners

9.   Production, fixed assets and real estate (if applicable)

9.1   General ledgers

9.2   Description of the facilities:

    9.2.1   Site plan (with surface) and location

    9.2.2   Indication of possibility for extension

9.3   List of all major items of equipment and machinery

9.4   Copies of all hire purchase, rental and/or lease agreements with respect to the equipment and machinery

9.5   Description of the owned real estate (if any) or rented facilities

9.6   Description of real estate leased, under concession or used under other rights and copies of relevant agreements

9.7   Copy of all administrative permits and licenses required by law for conducting the business

9.8   Copies of significant correspondence between the Company and the authorities during the last 3 years regarding permits and licenses, and list of inspections conducted by the authorities regarding compliance with applicable regulations

9.9   Any other permit, license, approval, certificate

9.10   Description of production process

9.11   Current status and operational capacity of production machinery

9.12   Current and envisaged investment projects

10.   Information technology

10.1   Description of operational IT-systems

10.2   Current status of IT-systems and MIS used (group, per country, per site), including details of the computer system used by the whole group

10.3   Current and envisaged IT projects

10.4   Overview of proprietary and licensed software and description of intellectual property rights over software developed in-house

10.5   IT organization chart including contracts

10.6   Copies of all agreements relating to computer systems, including computer software licenses, software development agreements and hardware leases, and any other long-term hardware procurement arrangements entered into by any of the companies

10.7   Network infrastructure and diagrams for each location and interconnectivity

10.8   Overview of IT development projects (details, budget, in-house or outsourced, etc.) with technology roadmap for the next 5 years

11.   Intellectual property and other intangible assets

11.1   List of all copyrights, patents, trademarks, trade names, domain names and logos owned or used by the companies indicating the nature of the title conferring the benefit (ownership, license, sub-license, etc.)

11.2   Copies of all registrations of and applications for registered trademarks, patents copyrights inclusive of designs and models owned or used by the companies

11.3   List and description of any infringements, claims filed, pending or threatened over the last 3 years, including assessments of the likely outcome concerning intellectual property

11.4   Description of any restrictions to the ownership and use of the intellectual property (e.g. is there any software written by employees with an independent statute)

11.5   Circumstances in which intellectual property rights, licenses or agreements may be lost (change of control provisions, etc.)

11.6   Describe R&D activities and management

11.7   R&D projects and budgets/capex over last 3 years

11.8   Details of quality insurance management, including policies, procedures, manuals, certificates and relation to the authorities

12.   Human resources

12.1   Staff

    12.1.1   Group management

        a.   List of members of the general management

        b.   Short CV of the members of general management and other key managers

        c.   Management structure

        d.   Details of all contracts with directors/connected persons and any 'related party' transactions, including loans between the company and its directors/managers or connected persons

    12.1.2   Copy of standard employment contracts in different countries

    12.1.3   Information on the use of 'interim' workers, freelancers and subcontractors

    12.1.4   List of description of all legal actions, claims, charges, pending or filed by social security or other government bodies

12.2   Functional organigram

12.3   Data per staff member

12.3.1 Job description

12.3.2 Skills (experience, certification ...)

12.3.3 Compensation and benefits: details of commission or bonus plans, stock option or stock purchase plans, any other profit sharing schemes, year-end premiums, company car, special leaves, luncheon vouchers, extra maternity benefit schemes, mobile phones, laptops, representation allowances, transportation allowances or any other remuneration, etc.

12.3.4 Details of invalidity insurance and/or other medical insurance

12.3.5 Date of birth

12.3.6 Number of years in service

12.3.7 Status (management, employees, workers)

12.3.8 Details of pension schemes, including type of scheme, eligibility, pension entitlements, fund managers, actuarial valuation of the funds, employee contribution, employer contribution and accounting treatment

12.4 Working regulations

12.4.1 Indication of applicable joint committee

12.4.2 Copy of applicable Collective Labor Agreements

12.4.3 Copy of internal working rules

12.5 Social relations

12.5.1 Status of social relations including strikes or other similar actions over the last 5 years

12.5.2 Description of works' council, trade union and other representation bodies within the companies

12.6 Description of all material legal actions, claims or charges, pending or filed by or on behalf of employees or former employees of the group during these last 3 years as well as any planned dismissal

12.7 Copies and details of potential social plans or redundancy scheme as well as provisions related to potential reorganizations

12.8 Details on training programs

12.9 List of service agreements or consultant contracts with annual fee in excess of 30,000 euros

12.10 Details of any outsourcing agreements

13.   Insurance

13.1   List and copy of all material insurance contracts taken out at group level or subsidiary

13.2   Overview of claims made over the last 3 years / pending

14.   Tax

14.1   Copy of the complete package of all tax returns of the last 4 years

14.2   Description of the tax position

14.3   Details regarding enquiries, questions that can lead to claims from the tax authorities. Date and remarks made during the last tax control

14.4   Pending discussions with the tax administration (VAT and income tax) / rulings obtained

14.5   Details related to potential deferred taxes

14.6   Overview of grants received and to be received

15.   Litigation/legal

15.1   List of company's lawyers and their roles

15.2   Copy of information provided by lawyers to the auditors for preparation of the annual accounts of the last 3 years

15.3   Overview of litigation:

15.3.1   Overview and details (including written pleadings) of all pending litigation for which the amount at stake exceeds 10,000 euros

15.3.2   Overview of all litigation or disputes with public authorities or third parties regarding the granting or challenging of public-law permits, permission or concession currently pending or closed or finally settled during last 5 years

15.3.3   Information about any threatened litigation in excess of 10,000 euros

15.4   If applicable, details of breaches related to permissions agreement or concessions

15.5   Description of contracts that include 'change of control' clause and/or non-compete clauses

	Internal approval	External approval (after internal approval)
Sales		
Standard contract	CFO + CEO	Head of sales
Standard contract	Head of sales	Head of sales
Amended contract	CFO	Head of sales
Standard non-disclosure-agreement (NDA)	Head of sales	Head of sales
Amended non-disclosure-agreement (NDA)	CFO	Head of sales
Request offer/tender/RFP	Head of sales + CFO + CEO	Head of sales
Credit note (without depreciation)	Accounting	Accounting
Credit note (with depreciation)	Accounting + CFO	Accounting
Purchases (OPEX)		
Budget < 1,500 euros	CFO	Everyone
Budget 1,500 - 5,000 euros	CFO	CFO
Budget > 5,000 euros	CEO	CFO or CEO
Outside budget 0 - 5,000 euros	CFO	CFO or CEO
Outside budget 5,000 - 25,000 euros	CEO	CFO or CEO
Outside budget > 25,000 euros	Board	CEO
Expenses	CFO	/
Investments (CAPEX)		
Budget 0 - 25,000 euros	CFO	CFO
Budget 25,000 - 100,000 euros	CFO + CEO	CEO
Budget > 100,000 euros	Board	CEO
Outside budget	Board	CEO

	Internal approval	External approval (after internal approval)
Bank transactions		
Payments up to 10,000 euros/week	Accounting	Accounting
Payments up to 50,000 euros/week	CFO	CFO
Unlimited payments	CEO	CEO
Bank cards and limit setting	CFO + CEO	CFO or CEO
Bank-to-bank transactions	Accounting	Accounting
Opening/closing of accounts	CFO + CEO	CFO or CEO
Loans		
Assets as guarantee	CEO	CFO or CEO
Other guarantees	Board	CEO
Personnel		
Vacancies	CFO + CEO	CFO or CEO
Appointing personnel	CFO + CEO	CFO or CEO
Dismissing personnel	CFO + CEO	CFO or CEO
Salary adjustments	CFO + CEO	CFO or CEO
Other		
Company taxation and legal structure	Board	CEO
VAT returns	Accounting	Accounting
Tax returns	External accountant	Accounting
Annual report	External accountant	External accountant
Compensation and benefits plan	CFO + CEO	CFO or CEO